YOUR KNOWLEDGE HAS VALUE

- We will publish your bachelor's and master's thesis, essays and papers

- Your own eBook and book - sold worldwide in all relevant shops

- Earn money with each sale

Upload your text at www.GRIN.com
and publish for free

Youssef Alyousef

National Identity in Irish Drama. A Study of Selected Plays by Yeats, Synge and O'Casey

Extended Version with Ten Plays And Broad Discussion

GRIN Publishing

Bibliographic information published by the German National Library:

The German National Library lists this publication in the National Bibliography; detailed bibliographic data are available on the Internet at http://dnb.dnb.de .

This book is copyright material and must not be copied, reproduced, transferred, distributed, leased, licensed or publicly performed or used in any way except as specifically permitted in writing by the publishers, as allowed under the terms and conditions under which it was purchased or as strictly permitted by applicable copyright law. Any unauthorized distribution or use of this text may be a direct infringement of the author s and publisher s rights and those responsible may be liable in law accordingly.

Imprint:

Copyright © 2015 GRIN Verlag GmbH
Print and binding: Books on Demand GmbH, Norderstedt Germany
ISBN: 978-3-656-91013-8

This book at GRIN:

http://www.grin.com/en/e-book/293141/national-identity-in-irish-drama-a-study-of-selected-plays-by-yeats-synge

GRIN - Your knowledge has value

Since its foundation in 1998, GRIN has specialized in publishing academic texts by students, college teachers and other academics as e-book and printed book. The website www.grin.com is an ideal platform for presenting term papers, final papers, scientific essays, dissertations and specialist books.

Visit us on the internet:

http://www.grin.com/

http://www.facebook.com/grincom

http://www.twitter.com/grin_com

Table of contents

I- Acknowledgement   3

II- Introduction   4

III- The Countess Cathleen   7

IV- Cathleen Ni Houlihan   44

V- Purgatory   69

VI- Riders to the Sea   85

VII- The Playboy of the Western World   105

VIII- The Well of the Saints   144

IX- Juno and the Paycock   162

X- The Plough and the Stars   181

XI- <u>The Shadow of a Gunman</u>   208

XII-<u>The Silver Tassie</u>   217

XIII- Conclusion   232

XIV- Works cited   236

Acknowledgement

This book comes as a continuation to the previous book with the same title, but this time, with ten plays and a broader discussion of the previously discussed ones. In this book, many specialised people have worked hard in order to answer the ongoing debates in the literary field. My deepest thanks go to all these people, to our friends, families and acquaintances. Thanks for them all, and again, thanks for those who made the composition and publication an event and not only a dream.

Introduction

The Irish national identity as portrayed in the dramatic works of the most prominent figures in Irish drama is the main theme of the following pages. The plays have been analysed while taking the national aspect as the main theme without avoiding the general line of argument. However, sometimes the general line of argument is suspended for a while in order to explain a branching theme but returns to converge with the main theme(s) of the play. What is to be taken into consideration during this analysis is the main theme(s). Certain national aspects are shown but not necessarily linked to the heart of the main theme. However, being themes about national identity aspects, make them go by their accord to the general theme of this dissertation. Moreover, in fear of repetition, some themes are used in order to substantiate a certain theme, but the supporting theme was mentioned earlier. This leads one to refer to the fact that each play cannot be understood unless looked at while taking the whole analysis of it into consideration. An example of this is <u>The Playboy of the Western World</u>; where historical facts converge with myth, language with psychoanalysis and all to be associated with the riots as something intended by the dramatist. In this dissertation, historical facts referred to in each play are mentioned, but loosely for reasons of being loosely selected. General theme of the play is analysed, followed by language use in each play. Psychoanalysis is also used and the whole analysis is associated to the general line of the play.

Most of the time, the least number of words is used in order to convey the most possible meaning. Therefore, sometimes the theme might not seem clear to the honoured reader, so one can refer back to the main source or continue reading; sometimes fuller explanations are used but in a more proper place. All this is used due to the lengthy information in the main sources and the complexity of the subject being discussed and above all not to go very far from the main line of the play to avoid confusing the reader. An example of this is Theosophy, where one source is about 500 pages, and the main themes of this religion are kept secret.

The dramatic works discussed are Yeats's <u>Countess Cathleen</u>, <u>Cathleen Ni Houlihan</u> and <u>Purgatory</u>, Synge's <u>The Playboy of the Western World</u>, <u>Riders to the Sea</u> and <u>The Well of the Saints</u> and Sean O'Casey's <u>The Plough and the Stars</u>, <u>Juno and the Paycock</u>, <u>The Shadow of a Gunman</u> and <u>The Silver Tassie</u>. Analysis starts with the title, the setting, historical events mentioned, the main source, symbolism, general theme, psychoanalysis, language, and finishing with associating the whole with the main theme of the play. Here are the main themes in these plays.

<u>Countess Cathleen</u> is mainly concerned with the return to Celtic-Buddhism through selling souls and language is poetic. <u>Cathleen Ni Houlihan</u> is mainly concerned with unifying the whole country by associating the wedding day with the day of independence. <u>Purgatory</u> is about political nationalism and cultural nationalism. <u>The Playboy of the Western World</u> uses the theme of

changing the world by word and the control of Christianity over the Irish id. Riders to the Sea portrays the rejection of Christianity for a place as small as a nail in Bartley's coffin. The Well of the Saints is about the ridge between romanticism and realism. The Plough and the Stars depicts the anti-nationalist as the most nationalist and the alleged nationalist to reveal his true self. And in Juno and the Paycock, the rejection of Christian control over the sexual power of the Irish. The Shadow of a Gunman is about romantic nationalism and realistic nationalism. Finally, The Silver Tassie is about political nationalism and cultural nationalism. Whenever words lose all their necessity, the argument stops, taking into consideration the highly experienced reader's ability to get the meaning in the least words possible. Moreover, the whole dissertation can be looked at as a kind of initiation; according to Victor Turner's theory, a developing character goes through three main stages: separation (Yeats's plays), transition (Synge's) and reincorporation (O'Casey's). Another thing is that the three dramatists represent another theory; romanticism can be turned into realism but one should cross the boundaries between them. Thus, Yeats represented romanticism Synge crossed the borderlines of romanticism (especially in The Playboy of the Western World) and O'Casey represented realism.

Countess Cathleen

The story of this play is old to a degree which makes it impossible to define the first source of it. However, it is most likely from the Druid times (Monaghan109). It is best, then, to take the story as a myth and deal with it as a well-known aspect of national identity. The story was altered by Christian influence, and Yeats added some details.

The play, set in the time of the Famine is highly national; the Irish blamed the British for the Famine. The Protestants' exploitation of the starving peasants' urgent need for sustenance, made them start their crusade for converting the Catholics into Protestants (Schulze 45, Howes 48, Harris 36). Moreover, the Irish looked at the British as the main cause of the Famine; God sent the blight and the British caused the Famine (Cusack 54). All these elements are loaded in the setting. The place is as in the real story, a peasant's cottage, which is the essence of Irishness. The characters are mostly the same as in the original story, except Aleel; he is Yeats, and before Yeats, he is the king of "Connaught" and his wife Maeve—who, assign Cuchulain as champion, and are well-known for judgments—are related to the mythical world of pagan gods (Monaghan128). The other elements of the play are the same as in the first version of the story. Therefore, it will not be needed to repeat the story, but it should be highlighted when the dramatist charges a new meaning into the general line of the play. The mentioning of an owl in the very beginning of the play, which does not exist in the main source, has a symbolic meaning; fairies. It was believed that they had the privilege of shape shifting (Monaghan 373). Moir goes to investigate Bridget's search for the meaning of the owl and comes to the conclusion that Bridget overlooked the behavior of owls; they hunt from the land but are aero creatures. In other words, the devils are unearthly (114). Shemus going to find work, and being expelled by the beggars are historical facts; during the famine, it was usual to see many beggars, but unusual to find work (McGreevy 65). After returning home, he mentions the death of all wild animals, in reference to the Famine, and labels the "badger" as one of the extinct animals. The badger is thought to be related to shape shifting while rats were thought to foretell death when they left a house, and related to prophecy and "precognitive power" (33, 391).

Aleel says to Shemus:

Shut to the door before the night has fallen,

For who can say what walks, or in what shape

Some devilish creature flies in the air, but now

Two grey-horned owls hooted above our heads (Yeats).

The poet was believed to tell prophecies. This is a foreshadowing to the coming of the two devils into the cottage.

Later on, Mary wonders why the devils do not give money to the starving people, they say that they know the "evil of mere charity". This is an allusion to the fact that Britain was reluctant to relieve the starving people in Ireland under the same pretext; the British Treasure Secretary was convinced that raising the income level of the poor would cause population increase, making the problem worse (McGreevy 12).

Cathleen.

A learned theologian has laid down

That starving men may take what's necessary,

And yet be sinless.

The learned theologian is Thomas Aquinas, who legislated for peasants taking food in order not to starve, and be sinless (Armstrong 18).

Cathleen orders her servants to bring all the peasants into her house and feed them until the house collapses. This is related to the fact that during the Famine, churches and houses were used to provide shelter and food (McGreevy 20). Moreover, she and the devils mention the coming of ships loaded with food. In fact, food was imported to Ireland from India. This is one of the reasons, though farfetched, which explains why the merchants wear Eastern clothes and sit in an Eastern manner. Moreover, the play mentions the theft of

Cathleen's property in addition to the devils' conversation about the expected arrival of oxen and grain in three days. Number three is mostly used due to the belief of being lucky. However, the historical fact is the export of cattle and grain from Ireland during the Famine (McGreevy 45, Harris 20, and Cusack 108). These were the historical details mentioned in the play. Now one can move on to the general analysis.

Firstly, Shemus and Teig are pouring blasphemous words on God, and all the characters are reading bad omens in the general atmosphere in the play; owls with human faces, death of badgers, thunder and hen's fluttering. Mary is concerned about Shemus's safety because supernatural spirits haunt the woods. When the devils enter, Mary's prayers avail her nothing. Even worse, she faints in front of the devils. They remind her that she will be starving in no time, and that they will be to her side in order to buy her soul. The comparison of God and devil is depicted as if devil is more generous than God! To understand this seemingly blasphemous comparison, one has to remember that the pagan gods were demonized in the Christian religion. Therefore, the whole thing is turned upside down; the devils are the pagan gods who came to reclaim the Irish's souls. If Yeats did not intend this, then it is meant to be in the same line of traveler drama, where a traveler comes to the community, alters some features in them, and leaves. By looking into the two above ideas at the same time with the fact that a devil is a representative of paganism opposing Christianity, one can return to the general line of argument. The devils buy the soul not for being a normal one, but for being religious. This means that buying the souls is buying Christianity in them more than mere buying of souls. This can be clarified in reference to the way the price of the peasant's soul is determined; the more religious the soul is, the more price it is offered to be bought.

The merchants, in order to oblige more peasants, and Countess Cathleen with them, to sell their souls, they go and steal Cathleen's treasure houses. The devils do not carry the bags, but use spirits to carry them. These spirits dance and sing. This is related to the world of the fairies; where it is believed that the fairies always danced and sang (Monaghan 300). Aleel the pagan poet speaks of such heavenly-like place during his unavailing attempts to relieve the Countess from her burdens. These burdens are held by Cathleen due to her Christian belief in her commitment to help the poor. The clearest manifestation of this argument is when Aleel comes to the devils in order to take his soul for nothing. They declare their inability to take Aleel's soul; he mocks their weak powers (compared to his) and even he puts fear in the devils' hearts. The devil kisses the circlet where his master's lips touched the circlet to pacify his frightened soul. However, when Oona and Cathleen come, the devils are at their work and their souls are calm. Countess Cathleen sells her soul and her soul quickly leaves her body, while the other peasants' sold souls are still within their bodies. This means, the more one is religious, the more they are vulnerable to devils. This idea is well established in the play I suppose. However, in Christian belief, the more one is religious, the more they are protected from the devil. While the case is the opposite in Yeats's play. This means that Christianity is what made the Irish soul and even body, so weak. Cathleen sells her soul, but this is a violation of Catholic belief (Schulze 40). This means that the general line of the play is meant to show, though dimly, that Christianity is vulnerable in Ireland compared to pagan culture. That is why Yeats added Aleel to the early version of the story. Countess Cathleen being saved by God depending on Christian belief is meant to be a violation of Catholic belief and not to validate Catholic belief. Moreover, it was thought that sacrificing one's soul for a general cause during a famine was applauded and national in Celtic myth: "…the Celts believed in **reincarnation**, the ritual offering of a human life to attain a community good, such as relief from plague or famine, might have been seen as a noble way to die"(Monaghan 464). When one follows the word in bold in the Celtic myth, he finds its relatedness into the Hindu belief; the dead person is given a new body when his body is dead (410). This might explain why the merchants are dressed in an Eastern manner and sit in an Indian method; on a carpet with crossed legs. This might be associated with the fact that Yeats was well aware of Eastern beliefs. Therefore, the merchants/devils influenced the community, and left them more pagan than before.

As for God saving Cathleen, it is noted earlier, that the Catholics who attacked the blasphemy in the play, wanted Cathleen to be sent to hell. Hence, it is her pagan belief which was responsible for saving her soul; she sold Christian belief. To stop a while in this point, it is well established that the buying of souls is connected to the degree of religious devotion; buying souls parallels buying Catholic religion/belief. If Countess Cathleen sold her belief in Catholicism, she would be left with paganism. Selling Catholic belief, and being rescued by the same religion she had sold, is unacceptable even if one left the decision to God; Teig, then, was right to indicate very early that there is no use in praying. God, nullifying the first side of the contract, devils would nullify the second. No money, then. Therefore, Countess Cathleen followed Aleel's advice to run to the world of pagan gods away from poverty and Christianity, by selling her soul to the devils, who were gods in the eyes of pagan Ireland. If it is not the case, Cathleen is in heaven as a reward for her sacrifice. This is again Aleel's advice in an altered way. Moreover, Cathleen's last words about a storm taking her away is related to Celtic myth: Bramsbäck argues that "…the last line that she utters 'The storm is in my hair and I must go' incorporates the belief that whirlwinds are associated with fairy troops and demons in the air" (Pamukova 44). Cathleen' foster mother— foster mothers mostly are linked with prophecy— Oona also "resorts to folklore imagery as well. Bramsbäck suggests that she, upon uttering 'crouch down, old heron, out of the blind storm', is depicted as if she were an ancient druidess"(Pamukova 43). Moreover, herons are thought to be linked with the other world power (Monaghan 262). Even Mary is associated with the Celtic myth by her hen; "On farms in the Scottish Highlands, a woman who kept chickens was believed to have magical powers and thus to be associated with witchcraft" (261). Hence, the play is about a pagan poet and his symbolic wife, (Aleel is a pagan king whose wife is Maeve, whom he mentions in the play), and a pagan foster mother, metaphorically speaking, living in a pagan community, with Christianity as a surface reality. The Protestant crusade and the intended Famine made the Irish go out of the crises as more pagan; more national.

Holding this in mind, one can return to the play. When Aleel is ordered by Cathleen to bring the devils, they attack him with a knife, but it hardly affects him. This is Christianity assassinating pagan world and culture in Ireland. Aleel is almost a pagan god; he is a poet—poets occupied a high social level in Celtic myth—being a poet means he is able to change the world by his words, prophesy the future, in addition to being a king. Moreover, he prophesied the future many times in the play: firstly warning Shemus from the danger of leaving the door open, then he curses the house which hindered him from prophesying about Maeve. Later on, he advises the Countess "But the dance changes. Lift up the gown, all that sorrow is trodden down."

The song literally 'invites both Aleel and Cathleen to join in the dance' that 'symbolizes the cycle of rebirth going on eternally', and which expresses his 'spiritual and physical longing for Cathleen [...] as well as the esoteric dance of death in which mortals join with immortals', thus representing the immortality and the endurance of the Celtic, and the ephemerality of the Christian world (Pamukova 42).

Finally, Aleel sees visions of hell after Cathleen has signed the contract. Before one moves to interpret Cathleen's speeches and their relations to pagan belief, it is best to quote "Cathleen's acknowledgment of Aleel's dedication and his greatness over hers stand as the most powerful recognition of Celticism":

God's procreant waters flowing about your mind

Have made you more than kings and queens; and not you

But I am the empty pitcher.

The "empty pitcher" is associated with Celtic myth; it was believed that a certain cauldron was used for revitalizing/ resurrecting dead warriors. Even more, her assimilation of herself to an empty pitcher is thought to be associated with the myth that a certain goddess impregnated the dead warrior to give him rebirth again. The goddess' name was Cymidei, who was regarded as a cauldron herself (Monaghan 308). The cauldron was also offered as a gift to the otherworld power (96). What can be taken from the lines in the play is that Aleel is wisdom and Cathleen is the cauldron. The wise god will fill the cauldron and the cauldron will multiply this wisdom. This is a beautiful image of wisdom kitchen, to counterpart soup kitchens run by the Protestants, in order to convert the Catholics into Protestants. This time, all the Irish can eat pagan wisdom, and convert into pagan belief. Even the relationship of a cauldron and wisdom has its roots in Celtic myth; a goddess used a cauldron to cook food and all those who ate her food were filled with wisdom (96).

George Cusack clarifies the reliance on pagan and Christian beliefs by the most religious characters to justify their immunity against the devils (56). However, Mary and the Countess are not away from the devils' hands. Even worse, the characters needed the pagan wisdom in order to prophesy the future, while Christianity is seen helpless in front of the devils. Moreover, Cusack mentions the breaking of Virgin Mary's shrine (which was deleted in this version of the play) and the falling of the shrine when the devils come. If this is found in an earlier version of the play, it goes with the general argument that Christianity is vulnerable in front of the devils' power, whereas it proved its weakness in front of pagan belief. Virgin Mary's statue, which is supposed to be a devil repellent, was broken due to the presence of a devil. The pagan poet, Aleel, who is supposed to be the most vulnerable character in front of the devils, is almost immortal and puts fear in the devils. Thanks to Cusack; this comparison was sparked by his analysis. Maybe in a previous version, Harris comments on the devil's speech reporting how he killed the priest. The devil, disguised as a pig, goes and knocks the priest dead (38). The priest being killed by a symbol of corpse eater, is something related to animal instinct; the priest is about to die. Therefore, the pig/devil killed him. The priest, as a representative of Catholic belief or Christian belief in general, is very weak in front of the pig/devil. Christianity is spiritually and physically vulnerable. It is reported during the famine, however, the death of some people by animals (Harris 38).

One has to return to the reasons given by the angles to justify Cathleen's deed. The angle says that God "looks always on the motive, not the deed" the motive is the sacrifice for the peasants in order to have a better life. This is related to Christianity and need not go to further the point as it is well-known. However, the Celts believed that the sacrifice for the general cause, especially during "plague and famine" is regarded as a noble death. The Celts also believed in the otherworld as being a Christian-heaven-like place. This is a motive for sacrifice too. Therefore, it is very little left for Christianity in Countess Cathleen's death and redemption. What is left for Christianity in this death and salvation is— that Countess Cathleen did not sacrifice her soul on Christian principles, or by following Christ's example, but— the similarity between the two beliefs concerning this sacrifice. Being national/ heroic and noble in both beliefs, it was accepted in Ireland. This gives the upper hand to pagan belief since it is older and the deed is pagan while the motive is both pagan and Christian. The third is left for Christianity, if calculated, and two thirds for paganism. The female figure sacrificing herself is a pre-Christian theme, too.

Concerning language, though it can be elaborated, it is better to be satisfied with one example and generalize the idea all over the play: Joyce was deeply impressed by the chanting of the lyrics, "Impetuous Heart" by Farr as Aleel, and especially "Who will go drive with Fergus now," chanted "with the thin voice of age" by Anna Mather as Oona:

Who will go drive with Fergus now

And pierce the deep wood's woven shade,

And dance upon the level shore?

Young man, lift up your russet brow,

And lift your tender eyelids, maid,

And brood on hopes and fears no more.

"As Richard Ellmann describes the effect of the lyric on Joyce, 'its feverish discontent and promise of carefree exile were to enter his own thought, and not long afterwards he set the poem to music and praised it as the best lyric in the world.' " (Schuchard 4)

As for the poem, it represents one of the most fantastic poems in the world. It mentions the unity of two lovers' souls in a spiritual world, where there is no need for fear or hope; it is heaven. When one remembers these lines, it comes to his mind the essence of life; knowledge. In uniting the two souls together, this means uniting the religion and exchanging wisdom. Uniting the religion cannot be achieved until the Countess converts into paganism; in other words, this is a Buddhist belief. More precisely, a Buddhist-Celtic belief. To substantiate this argument, one has to quote that 'in that island [Britain], the Druid priests and Buddhists spread teachings concerning the oneness of God, and for that reason the inhabitants are already inclined toward it [Christianity]' in the same line, here is a supporting theme for the previous quotation "Origen asserted in his mid-third century commentary on Ezekiel how that land had 'long been predisposed to' the tenets of Christianity, 'through the doctrines of the Druids and the Buddhists, who had already inculcated the Unity of the Godhead' "(Murphy 12, 13). If this is not enough to substantiate the argument, one can quote Yeats's students' comments during the play "we want no Buddhing Buddhists!"(Murphy 14). Then, one can return to the final lines of the play, where he finds Aleel seizing an angel to confirm that Cathleen is in heaven. As if Aleel is saying, if God did not send Cathleen to Heaven, we would not recognize God's authority on us; the Irish. In other words, if Cathleen was not sent to Heaven even though she is now Celtic-Buddhist, we would not embrace Christianity as a religion adopted by the Irish. That is why Aleel kneels in the end of the play; now, after Celtic-Buddhism is recognized by God as an acceptable religion, we, Celtic-Buddhists, can tolerate Christianity.

Yeats, therefore, went very far into the deep roots of history to bring the real land on which Christianity flourished. In doing so, he made clear that the Christianity is newer than what was known in Ireland, and that Christianity based its principles on older ones which dated back to Celtic-Buddhism in Ireland. Therefore, the selling of one's soul is not a betrayal of the country, as it was recognized by my first encounter with two books quoting each other (Schulze 40); otherwise Cathleen would not sell her soul even to relieve her people and be treacherous to the country she had sacrificed for. Selling the souls in this play is a return to pre-Christianity, which, for Yeats, is a revival of national identity.

Moreover, some go to distinguish between Cathleen's selling and the peasants'. It cannot be that a peasant selling his soul is condemned to be a treachery, and celebrate the leader's selling of her soul as a national deed. Some others argue that Cathleen sells her soul for the peasants, while they sell their souls to get money. In selling her soul, Cathleen has sold Ireland's soul to pre-Christianity, and in doing so, the peasants need not sell their souls to anybody after that. That is why the devils need Cathleen to sell her soul and are not interested in individual selling of souls, and when they get her soul back to pre-Christianity, they free the already sold souls. In other words, this is an individual identity, versus national identity. When one buys the national identity, he does not need an individual's soul. However, to make it clearer, when the national identity is returned to pre-Christianity, no need to return every individual's soul to pre-Christianity; Ireland's national identity is restored and that is what Yeats is concerned about. Ireland's national identity is revived by a return to pre-Christianity in Ireland, and now Cathleen/Ireland, is in heaven. The famine is substituted by heaven and Christianity is replaced by its predecessor; Celtic-Buddhism.

When one returns to the setting to find that the land is "famine struck" and ends in heaven, he has to think of Christianity as the main cause of this famine. Now Christianity can leads itself to Britain. Here is the place where Yeats accuses the British of causing the famine; Christianity is a religion but associated to Britain.

Gold for souls is to parallelize the real Irish national identity to the glittering gold. Moreover, Yeats intents to say that we, the Irish, have a national identity that deserves to be bought by too much gold. To rephrase it more precisely, selling the souls is regaining national identity. In selling the souls/Christianity, all the Irish are united; nothing now can divide them. Protestant and Catholic beliefs stem from Celtic-Buddhism, and Celtic-Buddhism is the essence of Irish identity. In this belief, all beliefs and folklore are congregated in the same cauldron. Now the cauldron can multiply food and wisdom, and Ireland is a heaven-like place. In this way, one can see the traces of occupation on Ireland; a new religion and an intended famine.

Yeats, it seems, intended the surface reality to be the opposite of deep reality. In this way, he shows the audience that Ireland's surface reality is Christianity, but the real fact is that Ireland is Celtic-Buddhist. Therefore, Yeats wants to indicate, it seems, that we (the Irish), will sell our souls to the devil and in doing so, we have money and regain our national identity.

When one ventures to wonder what it means in all beliefs, or even broadly speaking, in all cultures, to sell one's soul. It is selling one's belief. In selling one's soul, he returns to a previous cultural/ religious phase. It is abandonment of religious rites and embracement of bodily needs/desires. This is the id in Freud's psychoanalysis; since religion and norms are the main obstacles in front of the fulfilment of the id's desire. Religion and customs/norms are the ego. When the ego diverges, a retreat into the id is needed in order to redirect the wrong way of the ego: the ego is formed in a later stage, developing out of the id. More accurately, the id is the default version of any human being. What makes us different from each other is how the id is taught to suppress or confess some identity features. When one needs to correct a divergent characteristic feature, he has to return to the id, and redirect the wrong feature, to make it appear as an accepted characteristic feature. Therefore, Yeats went with the Irish, in his play, to the id (entity) in order to correct the foreign aspects in the Irish national identity. To use technological terms, when one's mobile phone does not work properly, he resets all previously readjusted settings into default mode.

The Irish state was confused by contradictory beliefs, so the best way to build a national identity is to unite the divergent aspects of this identity into one, and make it a national identity. Moreover, selling the soul deprives this soul of anything not in its essence. Then, when Countess Cathleen sold her soul, in fact she had sold all the fake aspect in this soul; Christianity. He intended to say that Catholicism, Protestantism, and Celtic-Buddhism worship one God and all converge in pre-Christianity.

A final return to the angels' justification of Cathleen's redemption; God looks always on the motive and not the deed. The motive, mostly is not expressed to others; it is in heart, while the way one worships God reveals his religion. Therefore, believe in God in your heart, and no matter how you worship Him. Believe in God in your heart, and go on dancing forever like the fairies. In this way, the mortals and the immortals, represented by the fairy world (who were thought to be dancing endlessly) are united. The past and present of Ireland are now attached to each other, religions are restored to one (in the heart), and mortals joined the immortals in their happiness. As far as I know, dancing, to some Eastern societies, is thought to bring the dancer into unity with the universe, as Yoga. The unity with the universe brings peace to the psyche. Unity with the universe, is the feeling of unity with the divine power in this universe, or to strengthen the soul through the absorption of the power from the divine power, which is found in the universe, and can be obtained through the unity with the universe/cosmos. However, that was what I think. This is what Lee thinks:

In Yeats's retelling of Celtic folklore, the Sidhe embody the deathless spirit of Ireland, safeguard its ancient values, . . . These Gaelic divinities, sometimes referred to as the Children of Danu, are revered among the peasants, as 'the powers of life, the powers worshipped in the ecstatic dances among the woods and upon the mountains, and they had the flame like changeability of life, and were the makers of all changes'. They represent, however, not just the powers of life, but more accurately, the perpetual life-in-death and death in-life flux, which they express through continual dancing and whirlwind-like motions (20).

To sum up this lengthy, but necessary quotation is to say that dancing is a worshipping rite, used to unite one' self with the whole power of the universe, including the spirits and forces of life in addition to the real maker of change in this universe. The meaning of dancing being now explained, though briefly as much as possible, one can relate dancing to national identity:

Among the critics, only Mester infers a link between Yeats's dance imagery and nationalism. She states that Yeats's interest in dance was both 'patriotic and mystical': 'He went digging into the myths and legends of the pagan Celts because he felt modern Ireland's unity depended upon the creation of a common mythology (Lee 19).

The above analysis defends Yeats against the accusation of establishing classes in Ireland through indicating that Cathleen's soul is more valuable than the peasants' souls. Because in associating the Irish with the universe, he merges the boundaries between them, and even between the world of the fairies and the real world, in addition to religious divisions. Moreover, Cathleen's soul is Ireland's soul, and he needs a reasonable price to make the peasants live a few days after Cathleen's death in the audiences' imagination, and to release the already sold souls, indicating, in the devils' words "they slipped away from our hands while you were talking". In other words, Cathleen's soul is the collective soul, so the peasants' souls are small pieces, firstly bought individually and that is why they were not valuable, but when the whole nation's soul is regained, the price would be worth the price of all the peasants' souls together. Even if it is taken for granted that Cathleen's soul is really intended to seem more valuable, this is not a place for objection; the more the soul is national/ generous/ courageous and self-sacrificing, the more valuable it is. The rogue's soul is already in the devil's hand; devils need not pay for it.

The last point of argument is considering selling of one's soul as treachery. If this the case, Yeats's intention is that Cathleen's soul is more valuable because she is more nationalist than the other characters who sold their souls before. This means, the more the soul is nationalist, the more it is valuable. The more the soul is ready to sacrifice herself for others souls' future, the more it is valuable. I suppose that one would ask how Cathleen's soul is more national than the others' souls. Well, God is more Merciful than the devil, those who sell their souls to God, not to the devil, are the most nationalist people in this country. So Cathleen's soul sold for others' redemption is more national than the saved souls. Moreover, her soul is Ireland's soul/ identity.

To rephrase, Countess Cathleen did not sell her soul in the literal meaning of the word, but Ireland's soul is regained to the essence of its Celtic-Buddhist origins. This back-ward journey can be interpreted as a result of Cathleen's encounter with the travelers, represented by the devils. The theme of leaving the community changed is well-known in the Irish traveler drama. Most often, the journey is back to remote history, but it is meant to be a step into the future; for it is a psychological journey into history and not a real backward one: the ego, psychologically speaking, is suspended for a while, and the journey happens in the id which is the unconscious part of the brain. After the traveler leaves, the nation comes into consciousness again, but with more national identity awareness.

This time to conclude, the play is a neurotic-psychic operation; psychiatric treatment of the national identity of Ireland, accomplished by joining in the dance. The dance is a symbolic movement expressing physical and spiritual perfection. This perfection enables the dancer to feel his self being united with the whole universe. It seems very close in its meaning to sophist rituals done by Muslims in Turkey; they move around themselves to emulate the movement of the universe, thinking they can be indulged in the general movement of the cosmos. However, not all can do it; one has to be spiritually prepared for this.

During the play's performance, one of Yeats's students shouted "we do not need budding Buddhists!" this means that Celtic Buddhism was there in Ireland, and that the play has some traces of Celtic Buddhism. In Celtic Buddhism, the universe communicates with us through symbols and that we can get involved in this universe in order to prophesy the future. When one gets involved in the universe, he can be in touch with the dead as well as with the future, and be in a complete unity with the universe. This is what Yeats called the Unity of Being: in this stage the person has got a "physical and spiritual perfection"(Lee 4). "Yeats ... [defined] Unity of Being... as unity of Brahma and Self."(151 Swartz). Brahma is God and sometimes it means Buddha. Since it is in Ireland that Shamanism is thought to be a religion, it will be better to use the newly coined term Celtic-Buddhism to mean Shamanism, Druidism and Buddhism respectively. In this way, one can be in the safe zone concerning the debate about the real meaning of the round towers in Ireland, which most archaeologists define as hallmarks of phallic worship while others say they are just as diaries for Ogham; the Celtic language. At any case, Celtic-Buddhism can be a correct term at least concerning the plays being discussed especially when taking into consideration the triple meaning of the term.

The setting of the play is in Ireland and in old times. However, the first words of the play are about a famine striking the land. This means that the play has something related to the Potato Famine in 1840-5. "The graves are walking" refers to the Famine, and associates the living with the dead. Mary: "There is something that the hen hears." This means that Mary is associated with the world of fairies and prophecy (Monaghan 373). When Teig goes to the door, he says:

In the bush beyond,

There are two birds--if you can call them birds--

I could not see them rightly for the leaves.

But they've the shape and colour of horned owls

And I'm half certain they've a human face.

In Celtic-Buddhism, or specifically, in Shamanism, the most important theme is shape-shifting. Gods or fairies are thought to have the ability of transforming their souls into animals. These lines connect the world of fairies or otherworld (mostly the same) with this world. As for the symbolic meaning of the owl, it is most likely a reference to wisdom and shape-shifting. When Shemus returns, he mentions his failure to beg due to firing him by the other beggars, giving a hint to the number of beggars. He also mentions his failure in finding a work. These are historical facts concerning the period of the Famine.

Shemus. When the hen's gone,

What can we do but live on sorrel and dock)

And dandelion, till our mouths are green?

Eating the roots is important in the initiation of shamanic religion in addition to fasting. These lines also hold some reference to the Famine because it was a Potato Famine. Before the arrival of Aleel and the Countess, Shemus hears music. Music is also important in the initiation in Shamanism (Endl 1).

Aleel advises the family to shut the door before night falls. Poets were thought to be seers or druids and were thought to be in a high social level in Celtic tradition.

"A man dressed as an Eastern merchant comes in carrying a small carpet. He unrolls it and sits cross-legged at one end of it." (Stage direction). Being dressed in an Eastern manner and sitting crossed-legged means Buddhism. As for the carpet, in order to refer to the trade they are in. Moreover, travelers in Celtic tradition were traders with many things including carpets.

The entrance of the merchants/ devils marks the end of the first noble truth; suffering and the beginning of the second; end of suffering by stopping to crave. This is what is meant by Celtic-Buddhism the second noble truth. The end of craving means the end of suffering, which means the second and third truths are now complete and we are about to enter the fourth noble truth; the cessation of suffering; the eight fold path: "The elements of the Eightfold Path [are]: Right View, Right Resolve, Right Action, Right Speech, Right Livelihood, Right Effort, Right Mindfulness [and] Right Concentration." (Hanson 7).

Teig. I'll barter mine.

Why should we starve for what may be but nothing?

In this sentence, one can see the eight elements encrypted in it. This is the stage where the devils want all the peasants, firstly, to reach. Secondly, they need the Countess to reach this stage. When she comes to sell her soul, the interest in individual souls disappears. When the Countess sells her soul, this means the achievement of the highest degree of the eight fold path in Celtic-Buddhism for the peasants; all Ireland. In Theosophy, sacrificing oneself for saving many is justified and welcomed, especially if this sacrifice is to save the wretched from hunger, damnation or any other blight (Blavatsky 136). In Celtic myth, it is also welcomed to sacrifice for the general cause especially during famine which was done as a human sacrifice. The sacrificed soul was considered to be a noble one (Monaghan 147).

Being famine struck, means that the king has failed to fulfill his role. This is a direct accusation of the British authority of the responsibility about the Famine. There are several allusions to this fact in the play. First, by mentioning the coming of ships loaded with cattle and wheat. In fact, during the Famine, the cattle were exported in addition to the grain. The selling of souls is also an historical fact; the Protestants exploited the miserable situation in order to convert the Catholics into Protestants in exchange of soup (Schulze 34). In this meaning, one can add that in Ireland, all the peasants were Catholics whereas the landlords were Protestants. However, the Countess, being a landlord, did not prohibit her from alleviating the peasants' blight. Selling the souls of the peasants in addition to the Cathleen's, means selling Christianity in its two sects. Selling Christianity means a return to a pre-Christian era, where Celtic-Buddhism was availing.

Now one can see how the Countess reaches the eight fold path. Firstly, she knows of the trade and starts suffering in order to stop the trade. Next, she uses her wealth for feeding the peasants and her house as a shelter. Finally, she surrenders to the devils' commands for selling her soul. In Celtic-Buddhism, these are the four noble truths as follows: suffering due to craving, cessation of suffering due to the cessation of craving and the fourth noble truth with its eight components: right resolve, right action, right view, right mindfulness, right concentration, right livelihood, right speech and right effort. These stages happen simultaneously and without arrangement. All of them can be seen in the surrendering to the Providence and the resolve about selling her soul at the end. In this way, one can see that the merchants' aim is to take the Countess step by step to the four noble truths. This track is meant to be a return to Celtic-Buddhism. Being a backward journey means for Freud and Jung as a return to the id. Taking into consideration that the Countess soul is the nation's, one can see that the whole nation now has returned to the id; the national identity now is restored. Moreover, the nation is unified by associating the Countess soul with God.

Since the soul was considered as the essence of the person and selling one's soul was considered as a betrayal of the nation, by selling the Countess soul Yeats managed to restore the real soul of the Irish identity. The thing sold is not the soul itself, but the Christian faith. The Countess soul now is in the hands of God in Celtic-Buddhism. Seeing the nation unified, the Countess can rest in heaven. Taking into consideration the fact that Aleel is a pagan poet, it is well-known that this figure is a seer, poet and a druid. In this way, one can see how druidism, shamanism and Celtic-Buddhism are unified. As for Christianity, it is very weak in front of these beliefs. When the Devils attack Aleel, they hardly harm him. However, when the Countess comes to the devils, they were able to take her soul. When Aleel offers his soul for nothing, the devils are frightened and one of them kisses the circlet put on the other's head to pacify his soul. This means that Shamanism and Celtic-Buddhism are the same except the fact that Buddhism is known for meditation. From now on, the use of Celtic-Buddhism is not a danger anymore. To the utmost level, Celtic-Buddhism is the basis on which Christianity has been built upon. To clarify this theme in the play, Yeats portrayed Christianity as a surface reality while Celtic-Buddhism is the real belief. Praying has no value, but the cessation of craving is valuable; it is the end of suffering; the second noble truth. Selling the souls is a kind of stopping to crave. In this way, the suffering ends. By ending the suffering, one can enter the eight fold path. In shamanism, there is what can be called "the Trance". It can achieved by listening to the sound of the drum or any musical instrument. This thing happens at the end of the play when the audiences hear a sound of horns after the Countess' death. Oona, at the end of the play also utters the words "come on, old heron". Heron is regarded as a bird related to prophecy and otherworld inhabitants. Therefore, she mentions words that make her look like a druidess. In this way, the mission of the devils is complete.

When the Countess and the peasants were Christians, the devils appeared, but when they become Celtic-Buddhists, the angels take the command on stage. The angels, being seen by the peasants means that they can see unearthly creatures. This is the highest level of Buddhism; the initiand can know about the future and see spirits from the otherworld. The devils came from the underworld, the humans are in the middle world and the angels from the upper world. In this way, the three worlds are associated together in one aim. The Celts believed in these three worlds, and believed that they were linked to each other by the tree of wisdom. However, one cannot see any allusion to this tree, but is found in <u>Purgatory</u>. This means that the intended meaning is what is achieved by the Celtic-Buddhist after he/ she reaches the eight fold path; being in touch with the other world. The same is for the Shaman and the druid. A fact about the Celts, is that they do not know the devil, but Christianity came up with the term and the figure. Christianity demonized some Celtic gods and made them devils. In this play, Yeats restored their previous place, united them with angels in the same mission; stopping to suffer by stopping to crave and the Famine is over. The Famine was there due to the failure of the king to do his duty to the goddess of fertility. When he does his duty, the Famine is over. The death of the Countess made the soil more fertile once again. The message, is, therefore, unite with the universe and everything is solved.

In addition to Celtic-Buddhism, there is the ultimate myth. It was believed that when the land was famine-struck, the king's soul is disturbed. This theme was used by Shakespeare in his plays, particularly in Macbeth. This time, the disturbance in the soul is Christianity and nothing else. When the Countess gives away her belief in Christianity, and even violates it, the whole problem is arranged. If some protest against the conclusion that the selling is of Christianity, they can refer to the play where the pious souls were paid higher prices than the wicked ones. Moreover, the more pious the soul is, the more vulnerable it is in front of the devils. Then, pious soul is more valuable and more vulnerable. Hence, Christianity is vulnerable, but the pious soul is valuable. When taking the soul, it is piousness of this soul. Since not all souls are ready to be united with God; only the pious ones. To conclude, the bought souls are bought to be united with the universe due to their piousness and to make them stronger by selling the vulnerability in them.

The Countess, being the spokeswoman of the community, she represents the collective soul of this community. By choosing to sell her soul for the rest, this means the utmost level of selflessness. This means she is nearer to the end of suffering; to stop being selfish; craving, means the end of suffering in Buddhism. That is why her soul deserves more than the rest in addition to the fact of being representative of the collective soul. In fact, this is a universal theme; wherever one finds troubles and wars, disputes arise among the citizens. But when some of them decide to stop craving and choose to sacrifice for the rest, the problem is solved. Theme of sacrifice for a general cause is applauded in Celtic culture and Celtic-Buddhism in addition to the fact that Christ sacrificed his soul for a general cause. This is a unifying theme in the Irish culture. Moreover, it is national. To sacrifice your religion for a general cause is not applauded in Christianity. Therefore, it is a sacrifice for national identity.

In Shamanism, everything has a spirit. When the Countess is about to die, she says "the storm is in my hair and I must go." This is related to the belief that the spirits travelled on wind. Concluding by this sentence instead of the normal prayer before death means that the Countess is a Celtic-Buddhist believer completely. The mirror ordered by Oona before the Countess death is ambiguous. It might refer to the mermaids pictured holding mirrors, or to a goddess who could see everything by looking into a magical mirror or to the fact that this object was buried with the dead. Since it is ordered before the Countess death, this means, most likely, looking into the future. Aleel's breaking of the mirror is the end of his craving; he mentions the end of craving for the Countess after he breaks the mirror. Therefore, he has ended his cravings and ready to end his sufferings. Celtic-Buddhism mingles with druidism. Aleel and Oona mention their willingness to end their lives; Aleel:" And have no excellence but the great hour" and Oona: " that I would die and go to her I love". This is also a unity of the three beliefs; Druidism, Shamanism and Celtic-Buddhism. The angels telling the rescue of Cathleen and being kissed by Mary means the acceptance of this religion which the Countess has converted to. The justification of the Countess' escapement is that the Light of Lights looks on the motive not only the dead. The motive is the rescue of the peasants and the deed is the selling of the Countess soul. The motive is acceptable in Christianity in addition to being so in Celtic-Buddhism while the deed is a Celtic-Buddhist principle. This makes the sum to be two thirds for Celtic-Buddhism and one third for Christianity. Moreover, the motive is looked upon as Christian, while the deed is pagan or Celtic-Buddhist. Motives are in the heart, while the deed is visible. This means that Christianity is in the heart and Celtic-Buddhism is in the action. Faith is Christianity but the applicability for Celtic-Buddhism. This means the same God being worshipped by all, while self-sacrifice is based on Celtic-Buddhism as a kind of selflessness. Believe in God, and behave in Celtic-Buddhism. In this way, you keep national identity alive and become unified with the universe. Give your nation, even though it contradicts religion to sacrifice yourself; it is accepted by God.

It can be hinted to the myth where it was regarded as a kind of protest when someone was insulted to go to the house of his opponent and abstain from eating anything until the matter is settled. Yeats might be alluding to a kind of protest such as peaceful protest used by prisoners nowadays expressed by abstaining from eating until they are freed. This leads to the conclusion that this protest has Celtic-Buddhist roots. This is the first play by Yeats concerning national identity. In which he call for a peaceful protest for liberation.

In psychoanalysis, the id forms the ego. If the id is Celtic-Buddhist, this means the ego is Celtic-Buddhist too. This is what is meant by the words "the Light of Light looks on the motive and not only the deed". The motive is in the id and the deed is the ego. When the motive of the id is revealed through the action of the ego, this means that the person is the most primitive man. Moreover, all the nation has returned to the id stage and the id expresses its thoughts by the actions of the ego. This is the most stable, though seems primitive, soul. The id and the ego now are in harmony; no need of the ego to suppress the id's primitivism. Moreover, the ego performs these thoughts. In this way, the nation has restored its lost identity, unified and stable.

What is left in this analysis is the general line of the play. When the play starts, the argument is directly about the myth and foretelling of death, shape shifting and wisdom. An owl is the symbol of wisdom and always associated with wisdom and shape shifting due to the face it has; similar to the human face. The hen flutters afterwards to indicate the association of the family to the world of prophecy and magic. Teig mentions the fact of the Famine and sees two owls with the shape of human faces. When the father comes, one can learn more about the difficulty in finding work or even begging. The countess and her attendants arrive. Usually, the traveler changes the community, but this time the arrivals did not make any change. Moreover, the community is a community of beggars. Beggars usually were associated with tinkers; the dynasty which the Irish were thought to descend from. Moreover, the Countess and her followers are travelers and the community is a group of beggars. Later on, the real two travelers arrive. This time, they have something to tell. In Irish Culture, the beggars/ tinkers/ travelers are welcome always due to the fact that they have a lot of stories to entertain their hosts with. Moreover, when Mary faints, the Devils were quick in taking their comfort at the family's home. This is also an historical fact; it was known that when a family left her home, the tinkers who used to beg from this house hurried to search the house for food or anything valuable. Mary, being left with the two devils is something related to the Irish Custom. It was thought that one has to make his guest comfortable to the degree of honoring him to sleep with his wife as an extra level of hospitability. The two devils being merchants is an historical fact. Most tinkers were traders or metalworkers. Those tinkers used to sell many things including carpets. Shemus and Teig going from house to house is the way those tinkers sold their goods. This is the stage where it is thought to be the cessation of suffering in Celtic-Buddhism. In this phase, the person stops craving and surrenders to the Ultimate

Power. By stopping to crave, the suffering ends. When the suffering ends, the person enters the eight fold path. This stage was reached by the peasants and lastly by the Countess. Aleel, being a poet, this means that he has the ability to prophesy the future. He does so when he advises Shemus to shut the door, when he reads the omen of the owls hovering above them, seeing the battle between the angles and devils. He is also associated with the world of the fairies of which he speaks about most of the time. By associating Aleel to the Otherworld, the Countess is also associated. Therefore, Aleel is a medium by which the Otherworld can communicate with this world. This is the work of the poet, the druid, the Shaman in Celtic myth, and the enlightened person in Celtic-Buddhism. When Aleel advises the Countess to flee to the countryside, she refuses, but finally, she flees to heaven. This is Aleel's advice, but in an altered way. Instead of fleeing in order to have peace away from the miseries of this world, she sacrifices and by this sacrifice she is rewarded. In this way, she follows the Celtic-Buddhist teachings in giving all cravings instead of Aleel's advice which is Druidism. Aleel, Oona and the villagers all kneel in front of the angels as a kind of submission to the same God, which the Countess has fled to away from the misery in this world. It is the utmost unity which can be achieved in a nation. All the rest are willing to do the same as the Countess, but now things have changed; there is no need of a new sacrifice for the nation. The national identity is restored. The play starts with a famine, and ends with heaven. The characters were divergent at the very beginning and selfish. At the end, all are worshippers of the same God, and ready to follow the Countess and even to sacrifice themselves instead of her as one of the characters mentions. This is Celtic-Buddhism uniting the whole nation and turning the famine-struck land into a heaven. The message, is, therefore, stop to crave and be selfless in order to finish your sufferings. The motive being angelical and the deed being devilish is something to stop at. This means the id is now angelical and better than the ego. The ego is devilish and the id is angelical means Celtic-Buddhism is angelical and Christianity is devilish. Therefore, God accepts the deed as it is motivated by the Celtic-Buddhist id, performed in a Celtic-Buddhist way by the ego. Christianity is nothing at all in this sacrifice. Moreover, the id being angelical while the ego is devilish is the utmost level of return to the identity of a nation. The id, as it is well-known, is primitive and needy. Here, it is angelical in comparison to the ego. This means the id will make a new ego show up and eliminate the previous one, making of Ireland a Celtic-Buddhist nation instead of the previous ego of Christianity. In order to make the ego like the id, the nation has to make the surface religion Celtic-Buddhism.

The countess' bag is empty, her store house and gold are gone. However, she has her faith. In fact, this is the Celtic-Buddhist belief. These are the means by which the Countess is taken step by step towards the eight fold path. By taking her property, she has no craving. By taking the other peasants' souls, she begins to think of giving. Finally, she accepts to sign the contract. Then, the crisis begins with the famine, continues to the theft of the treasures and the climax is when the Countess has nothing but to starve if she did not accept the offer of buying her soul. In selling her soul, the Countess ceases to crave and is ready to tread the path. The countess property decreases and the Devils' property increases until the Countess has to sell the last fort to which she retreats; her religion. In this way, Yeats managed to make of selling the peasants their Catholic beliefs during the Famine as something national instead of being treason. By selling the Christian belief, they become Celtic-Buddhists. By making the Devils steal the Countess' property, Yeats alludes to the British stealing the Irish property in order to make use of the Famine for causes that are related to national identity. The Famine, in fact, had numerous effects on cultural identity especially in regard of religion, language and emigration.

Selling a soul is a conversion into a new religion. When the Countess knows of selling the souls, she uses the same means by which these souls were bought; money. When money vanishes, she sells her religion. By selling the Countess' religion, the whole nation converts into Celtic-Buddhism. However, Celtic-Buddhism is a religion known for meditation. Meditation requires fasting, suffering, stopping to crave and then the fourth noble truth or the eight fold path. That is why the thing happens in this way. Celtic-Buddhism is not taken as just a belief in something and everything is fine. Instead, it is like descending the stairs. Every time one has to pass through a stage until the end, where the path is.

In this play, one could have seen how Yeats managed to make one of the historical facts as something very national although its historical truth is vice versa. Yeats depicted the selling of souls as national during the Famine, and that the sold souls were sold to be followers of Celtic-Buddhism; the ground on which Christianity was based. In this way, he returned the nation to the id and the id projected a new ego. The world of the fairies or the dead, this world and the upper world were connected. This is also a Celtic-Buddhist conception. By selling the Countess' soul, the whole nation has done the same. Selling the soul is selling Christianity or conversion into another religion. When the Countess has reached the eight fold path, the whole nation did the same; her soul is the collective soul or the nation's soul. Soul and identity refer to each other for most of the time. Therefore, the soul or identity is restored to where it had been before Britain came to Ireland.

Cathleen Ni Houlihan

The name of the play is well-known to be an aspect of national identity as it turned to symbolize Ireland. The setting is Killala 1798, the place and date of a rebellion. In this year, the Irish started a rebellion leaded by Theodore Wolfe Tone after asking help from Napoleon. In this rebellion, there was an extreme use of violence in order to defeat the rebels. Killala is the name of the Bay to which the 1000 French soldiers landed (Bell 15). All these symbolic meanings associated to the setting are national; revolution, Wolfe Tone, and Killala. Moreover, the rebels, being Catholics, Protestants and Dissenters, make the rebellion more national.

Harris mentions some historical details related to post-Famine period such as Bridget's decision to make of Patrick a priest; celibate forever. This is associated with the fact that during the Famine, the Irish did not think much of marriage, and even considered it as undesired. If it was to happen, it was similar to Michael's and Delia's; she has land and money and Michael will inherit his parents' property. Buying the land was restricted to rigid rules/laws, and the case of Dempsey's death and Delia's dowry is an example of this restriction (Harris 56). However, detailed historical facts in the play need further study in Famine effects, post-Famine situation and Penal Laws, which are to be detailed later on.

The setting, being a peasant family cottage, makes the play go step by step with the notion of traveler drama; a genre recently discovered in Irish drama of the twentieth-century. The genre can be associated with national identity in relating the travelling theme with the idea of dispossessed peasants of their land, and the tinkers; the race from which the Irish descend. The play, then, is about a family living in the countryside—the essence of Irish identity, and the best place for the traveler's visit—arranging for the marriage of their son, and hearing some cries in the distance; most traveler drama action starts when the everyday life is suspended for a while. In these unusual incidents, the scene is about Bridget and Peter. The couple is to counterpart the new one, and Cathleen is the collective spirit. The wife and her husband discuss memories of their old marriage and the intentions for future, while they are busy in the present. Patrick mentions the horses fair and the horses taking water well. This is related to second sight in Celtic Myth. More precisely, horses were associated with the fairies' world. The day being unusual with too much cheering and loud cries makes it one of the best days when the otherworld inhabitants visit the real world in order to take somebody away.

In these circumstances, the Old Woman, the traveler, arrives. The family members try to discern their guest's identity. The ambiguity of the Old Woman's identity can be interpreted as related to Celtic myth. To the Celts, the distinction between historian, poet, judge and prophet were not distinct (Ebbutt 52).

Therefore, the Old Woman starts to reveal her true identity. She identifies herself with travelers in order to allude to the fact that she is dispossessed of her land. The Old Woman states clearly that her land was taken from her, and her land is "four fields"; four Irish provinces. Then, she mentions some of her lovers who died for love of her. In order to mention those lovers, she uses poetry. Poetry is associated with magic; metaphor is shifting in words, and magic is shape-shifting (Ebbutt 200). Poets were seen as seers of the future, and most of the time they were used to decide who would be the next king.

After using poetry, which is the medium by which the heroes are immortalized, she mentions some people who died for her. The Old Woman mentions people, it seems, from different parts of the country, associating those who died centuries ago with the recently dead and with the future dead. In this way, she introduces herself as caring for the people who died for her. By doing so, she reveals one of the goddesses' features; caring for the dead, and foretelling death (Ebbutt 30). Moreover, she unites the whole dead martyrs in the whole country, of all the successive generations together.

Bridget: "Is she right, do you think? Or is she a woman from the other world?" this is the first time in the play the Old Woman is associated to the otherworld. In this association, Yeats ties the two worlds to each other. Peter. "The poor thing. Give her some milk and an oaten cake." This offering of milk is also related to the fairies; where it was believed that the fairies loved drinking milk, and they might make one spill some milk in order to drink it (Ebutt 40). Bridget insists on giving the Old Woman some money in fear their "luck would run out of [them]" this is related to the period of the Famine, when it was thought that if "hungry man" was given money, it brought good luck to the house (Ebbutt 30).

The Old Woman mentions her untouched virginity. In this way, she has clarified herself as much as possible; she is Ireland, everybody knows this. But before she is Ireland, she is a goddess. Moreover, goddesses usually are known by their special professions, but the Old Woman has the features of a goddess but no distinct profession is associated to her. To rephrase the most salient features of this goddess, and each one with the explanation:

1- horses ↔ related to second sight and fairies who could ride them all the night.

2- Water ↔ a place where the otherworld inhabitants live.

3- Horse and water ↔ a magical horse associated with shape-shifting.

4- Milk ↔ fairies like it and come to steal it.

5- Poetry ↔ prophecy, shape-shifting, and fairies.

6- Virginity ↔ shape-shifting, and prophetic goddesses cannot tolerate pregnancy.

7- Foretelling of death ↔ prophecy

8- shape-shifting ↔ fairies and goddesses (Ebbutt 237).

Before the last feature is revealed, the Old Woman associates herself to Ireland. At the very time she is about to leave, the Old Woman reveals her name; Cathleen Ni Houlihan.

At this time, no one in the audience is still suspecting the Old Woman's identity since the name was very old, known to be used by poets as old as the ninth century, describing themselves seeing a beautiful woman in their dreams, and when asked about her name she answers that she is Cathleen Ni Houlihan, or the Poor Old Woman and more other names. This woman mostly was described as beautiful and in an urgent need of help. Grote traces the figure of Cathleen Ni Houlihan back to the "Bardic tradition of Gaelic-speaking poets", who loved Cathleen Ni Houlihan's beauty, even though they alluded to Ireland (23).

Again, there is no need of prayer as in The Countess Cathleen. Prayers, graves, food for the dead, keening and money for strangers, are all amulets to keep the fairies and the dead away. This time, they will come back and even be united with the living, as the still living Michael is about to join the dead in the otherworld. Cathleen Ni Houlihan prophesies many people's deaths, and even the money, which Michael brought home will not be used because Michael has joined Cathleen's lovers. Patrick states that he did no see an old woman, but a young woman, with the walk of a queen. This is shape-shifting, and it is related to goddesses. However, this transformation is not without a reason. It is well documented that poetry is associated with magic and shape-shifting. Goddesses and fairies also had this power. However, this transformation is due to a combination of more than one myth. It was believed that the dead warriors had a great peace if their bodies were soaked with a new blood. Blood, as the essence of life, was thought to revitalize the dead warrior into life once again "Blood may have been interpreted as bearing the essence of life force; thus drinking blood would restore the warrior" (Ebbutt 50). That is why the Old Woman transforms into a young woman; the dead rebels' blood has refreshed the old one, and now she is young once again. Some critics go to accuse the Old Woman of being a vampire. One has to remember that she is a symbol of Ireland. Land always drinks the martyrs' blood, but nobody calls the land a vampire.

Cathleen Ni Houlihan is Michael's metaphorical mother and metaphorical lover. In this case, Michael has two mothers like Cuchulain; a hint can be taken by putting his name and surname, and pronounced with little difference refer to Cuchulain: Mi Chaelgillane; my Cuchulain. When Patrick is about to leave in order to investigate about the cheering, Patrick asks Michael if Delia would remember to bring the dog. In Cuchulain's myth, after Cuchulain had slayed the dog, the hosts and guests went out to see what the cheering was for; it was due to Cuchulain's slaying of the dog. Michael and Delia's marriage is the finest to the priest. Also Cuchulain was the best among his comrades. Finally, both are warriors.

Michael, being in love with his metaphorical mother, might hint to Oedipus, but there is not much to say about this. However, it opens the argument of psychoanalysis. Freud mentions Oedipus's marriage to his mother to explain the innate desire of the boy to substitute his father in his duty to his wife. Moreover, this feeling, according to Freud, is due to the fact that the mother is the real female person who is close to the child. While later on, the boy searches to find a lady to fill the desire which was filled by the mother in a previous stage. However, in Freud's analysis, the closeness to the mother is related to the id, which was not yet suppressed by the ego (social norms and religion). After the ego is shaped, the young man no longer thinks of anything other than his sweetheart to the degree of forgetting his mother. Michael is a young man at the age of marriage, and has a fully grown personality. When the Old Woman comes, he goes, spiritually, to be tied to her. Therefore, Michael's encounter with the Old Woman made him go back to the id; where the boy's urgent need is occupying the father's place. Then, Michael has returned to his true self; to the id (entity). Michael is any Irish man. Michael's hesitation in taking a final decision in the end of the play is due to undetermined id(entity) has overcome the other; the id is supposed to ally with Delia, but now it has returned to a previous phase; the id is now tied to the mother. Finally, Michael's identity is restored.

Michael's decision to substitute the metaphorical father means his indulgence in a fight over the mother's body. This means Michael has to fight the British to get his mother/Ireland. Restoring Michael's mind into the childhood state means restoring the ids of the whole country. This means that all Ireland has returned to the id state. In this way, Cathleen Ni Houlihan returns young again. Cathleen Ni Houlihan goes out with the walk of a queen. This queen has no husband; she is free of the chains laid on her by the suppressive father. Ireland being restored to the id phase, means primitivism, where there is no religion to suppress the motivations of this primitive, desiring and needy id. Ireland's identity is restored. Finally, Cathleen's transformation, taking place in this way, means that Cathleen is not only Ireland, but more precisely, Ireland's national identity.

The language of the play is a place of debate. Some critics attribute the language of the play to Lady Gregory, except that of the Old Woman's. I suppose that the play would have been inconsistent if two dramatists had written separately; each one with his own language and symbolic references would have made the play's message confusing and even sometimes contradictory.

Therefore, it is only possible that Lady Gregory made the language a peasants' one. This can be validated by comparing the language of this play to Synge's

Bridget."…the boys would [be] laugh[ing] at you"

Peter. What is it you would [be] ask[ing] for?

Old Woman. …but when the trouble is on me I must [be] talk[ing] to my people

Bidget. I [do] [be] think[ing] sometimes,…

Michael ….where would they [be] go[ing]…

Patrick. …they [do] [be] cheer[ing]…

Michael. Is it long since that song was made? Is it long since he got his death?

Old Woman. That's true of you indeed, and it's long I'm on the roads since I first went wandering.

Peter. …I never thought…since Dimpsey died

Bridget. …and never asking big dresses or anything but to [be] work[ing].

Finishing with this sentence which uses two Anglo-Irish syntactic rules; the use of do+be+verb+ing with a variation of omitting "do" sometimes. The second rule is the avoidance of the present perfect tense where there is no alternative in Standard English as shown in these examples above. However, most of the language used is normal and is not related to Anglo-Irish language. This refers to the fact that both, Yeats and Lady Gregory were not in real touch with the peasants, or could not document, as Synge did. This argument can be substantiated by these examples from the play. Patrick....do be cheering....are cheering. Old Woman...they think old age has come on me....but when trouble is on me, I must be speaking to my people. Therefore, the hands which wrote the language were shivering; they had not mastered the real spoken language. Though this argument has no place in this dissertation, but seems true. The play was "made" to look "real" but the "reality" is that the language was an amateur imitation of peasants' language. As for poems in the play, they, surprisingly, have the same style:

Old Woman. I am come to cry with you woman/ I will go cry with the woman

....

Oh! We'd have pulled down the gallows

....

> They shall be speaking for ever

Thinking of the final line, one can notice that it is both Standard English, and an Anglo-Irish style, used for poetic language. Therefore, the language is poetic due to the use of Anglo-Irish style. To clarify this point, one can rearrange the final line to become: they will/ shall speak for ever. The same can be said about "I am come to cry with you woman" and "I will go cry with the woman"

The last lines of poetry spoken by Cathleen call upon the women "not to make a great keening", and not to pray for the dead. This means that the dead in old times needed to be mourned as a kind of reviving them into the present. While those who will die tomorrow are makers of freedom, so they will live "forever". Or it might be still deeper; the dead in old times did not achieve their aims of freedom, so they do not rest in their graves as Ireland is not free, while those who will die tomorrow will rest peacefully because they are expected to accomplish their mission. In this way, they need not be mourned.

Keening was invented by the goddess Bridget, after her son had been killed in battle. It is a Celtic ritual but not acceptable in Christianity (Ebbutt 286). The Old Woman invites the woman to abandon keening, and at the same time one has to take into consideration the similarities in names; the character Bridget and the goddess. This means that the Old Woman is inviting Bridget not to invent keening, not because keening is not accepted in Christianity, but because it will not be needed any more. It might be also that Michael is not going to die.

Yeats, after the Easter Rising, wondered if this play "sent certain men the English shot" Muldoon replies to Yeats's enquiry that the answer is "certainly not", and that history makes art not the other way round (Schulze 60). This dissertation is not going to answer a question which Yeats was not sure about, while Muldoon answered it with denying any relationship between the Rising and the play. However, to get the answer "right" is to go to Pearse's speeches, and see if there is something related to this play in particular, not to the Celtic myths in general. The lines are taken from O'Casey's play "The old heart of earth [Old Woman] needed to be warmed with the red wine of battlefield [transformation into a queen]…without shedding of blood there is no redemption", "they think they have pacified Ireland…while Ireland holds these graves, [they shall be remembered forever] Ireland, unfree, shall never be at peace." It seems that Mr. Muldoon has to pardon us; the answer is "right". Even one of the sentences echoes one of the Old Woman's and the two sentences are going to be put next to each other to see the similarity in them:

Pearse. …They think that they have pacified Ireland

Old Woman….when the people see me quiet, they think old age has come on me and that all the stir has gone out of me. …

There are more than these similarities, but they might have something in common with Celtic myth. For example, "who ripens in the hearts of our young men the seeds sown by young men of a former generation". For more about this topic, one can refer to Grote "Pearse modelled the speeches and actions of the Easter Rising on Yeats's play" (22). Anyway, attention is on the play's national aspects more than on its internalization by the Irish.

Cathleen Ni Houlihan, as a symbol of national identity, transformed into a young girl means a revival of the national identity. The same symbol being transformed, means the re-birth of this symbol. Michael's sacrifice for the sake of the country made him gain a place in Ireland's history in order "to be immortalized in the very traditions that distinguished Ireland as Celtic and not Saxon" (Grote 127). If Pearse is Michael, then, Cathleen Ni Houlihan was right to prophesy their immortality. Moreover, the play, being acted in real life, transforming art into reality, then reality into history, is something related to Synge's <u>Playboy</u>. O'Casey's plays always have the symbolic Cathleen Ni Houlihan in them. This means that this play influenced dramatists of the Abbey Theatre and the history of Ireland. This leads one to the conclusion that the Abbey Theatre and the recent history of Ireland formed each other. Of course,

Yeats's play is too theoretical; it needs a method of application. That is Synge's mission in his Playboy.

Now a final return to the play. Bridget weaves Michael's clothes. This is related to the Celtic myth, which indicates the fairies were skilful spinners and weavers, and criticized the poor skills in this world's women (Ebbutt 171). The sight of a woman knitting means she has magical and prophetic powers (290). When Bridget is annoyed by her husband, she reminds him of his property when she had married him "and a flock of hens" which associate Peter to the world of magic and prophecy too.

The day in which the Old Woman arrives is dedicated to preparations for Michael's marriage. This means the preparations for marriage are to represent the preparations for the rebellion, since Michael is any Irish man. Celebration for symbolic marriage between the nation and its people will take place in the next day. It is the Independence Day. Therefore, Yeats indicates that whenever the Irish national identity is restored, the Day of Independence will be close. In this way, Yeats intends to achieve a real historical event out of art. As mentioned earlier, this is Synge's intentions too. O'Casey, on the other hand, rejects the belief that words/ art/romance can change into reality or change reality, and satirized this belief. This contention has a Celtic root. Poetry, was thought to be able to change the physical world. A satirist poet could punish the king by his severe verbal satire, making him unable to rule any more (Ebbutt

35). However, one has to readjust his first impression when a mythical belief is mentioned, and not to conceive it as completely not true or unlikely to have anything related to reality. This does not mean that myths are real events which really happened. Myths, as I believe at least, have something related to real facts or incidents. Upon these events, stories developed, and interesting, but exaggerated details were added to add more suspense to the myth/story. One might not believe, for example, that the Fenians were real warriors in Ireland (198). Or again, Noah's wife as a pagan woman, who defied God's Will. Therefore, myths, being a mixture of religious beliefs, culture, customs, folklore and legends, make them bear some traces to reality. Moreover, it is well-known that all stories have moral messages, which are accepted all over the world. Nonetheless, words being able to change the real world, seems true in Ireland, but unacceptable elsewhere. Kearney, playfully, says that "if words could change the world, the Irish should have destroyed Britain long time ago" (10). Jung, it seems, is ready to answer such a question about the relationship between myths and reality:

A nice example that has been greatly discussed recently is the near-death experience. It seems that many people, of many different cultural backgrounds, find that they have very similar recollections when they are brought back from a close encounter with death. They speak of leaving their bodies, seeing their bodies and the events surrounding them clearly, of being pulled through a long tunnel towards a bright light, of seeing deceased relatives or religious figures waiting for them, and of their disappointment at having to leave this happy scene to return to their bodies. Perhaps we are all 'built' to experience death in this fashion (Boeree 5).

He goes on explaining the "archetype mother"; we all came to this world, and immediately cried for our mothers. This is related to the mother figure in our brain; even though we have not seen her before. I am obliged to quote another lengthy quotation, due to the perplexity of the subject being explained:

Even when an archetype doesn't have a particular real person available, we tend to personify the archetype, that is, turn it into a mythological "story-book" character. This character symbolizes the archetype. The mother archetype is symbolized by the primordial mother or "earth mother" of mythology, by Eve and Mary in western traditions, and by less personal symbols such as the church, the nation, a forest, or the ocean. According to Jung, someone whose own mother failed to satisfy the demands of the archetype may well be one that spends his or her life seeking comfort in the church, or in identification with "the motherland," or in meditating upon the figure of Mary, or in a life at sea (7).

Therefore, myths were invented to satisfy our unconscious need for something we could not find around us, but felt the need to fill the empty space that is allocated for it in our psyches. Jung explains the hero figure to be an imagined savior/ Christ, the search for the lady as an innate need to find our lost second half, the magic trickster putting obstacles in front of the hero, associations with animals as an image of the hero's faithful horse, and so on (7,8). Jung, therefore, went to use mythology in his psychoanalytical theory. He wanted to conclude, and I am afraid of Macbeth's "over leap" that our unconscious part of our brains contains all the incidents recorded by our forefathers, unconsciously. This means that our brains, the unconscious part particularly, contains the wisdom learned by all our predecessors. If this is the case, one poses the question whether scientific discoveries should be looked for by updating his information with the latest discoveries, or go back to myths. Personally, I think that a lot of knowledge is in our brain, but needs to be activated by reading. Otherwise, how one can explain making a new discovery, by reading somebody's work, and the author of this book did not discover what the reader found out. To conclude, taking my religious background into consideration, the knowledge in this world is installed by God in the human beings' unconscious part of the brain. The geniuses are those who discovered the hidden treasures in their brains.

To go back to the previously posed question about whether words can change the world, one can assume that it was stored in the human beings' brains that God can change the world by word! But because of the absence of religion in myth, this ability was attributed to poets. Moreover, word and science are related to each other on one hand, and science and changes in the world are also known on the other hand. Therefore, words can change the world.

The play starts with the stage directions telling of a cottage near Killala. These implications have been clarified above. What needs further illustration is the theme of traveler. When the Old Woman arrives, the family suspects her of being a tinker woman. Therefore, they offer her some money and milk. Peter, hearing of the Old Woman, goes to hide the money. The Irish usually welcomed the tinkers for the latters were usually full of tales which entertained their hosts. Moreover, the Old Woman starts to sing. This is also an idea taken from real life. Tinkers were musicians and singers. However, what is unusual is the begging for sacrifice. In Irish myth, there were warriors who roamed the country just for immortality, helping the kings to settle their affairs. Sometimes they were paid and mostly just for being remembered. Those were the Fenians. In this play, the nation is roaming the land symbolized as an old woman. The meaning of being disguised as an old woman has its roots in Irish myth. It was believed that it is safer to transform one's soul in the form of an animal or a human being than appear in the normal shape. This was the case for fairies and goddesses. As for the choice of an old woman, it is firstly safer, and closer to getting help. Another thing, the land was portrayed as a female with mountains as breast and rivers with milk in addition to the theme of fertility and birth. Another myth refers to a goddess who was able to impregnate the warrior and bring him back to life. The Irish thought of blood as the essence of life, and drinking the blood would restore the dead warriors into life once again. What is more is the fact that Yeats mingled all these myths into one, by making the nation old and in need of a new blood to renew its fertility. This means as long as the nation deserves—in the eyes of the Irish—self-sacrifice, it will stay young. For young men are always will be ready to sacrifice their lives for her sake. This means she is dearer to them than their brides because she is lovelier than any lady. The Old Woman chants the phrase "they shall be remembered for ever". In fact, the Irish believed in reincarnation in addition to the theme of human sacrifice in order to appease the gods. Many discoveries in bogs show that human sacrifice was not uncommon in Celtic culture. The chanted phrase "they shall be remembered for ever" also associates the world of the dead to the world of the living and the Old Woman had come from the world of the goddesses. This makes the complete unity in the nation. The three worlds are unified in one. One can remember Celtic-Buddhism, and being this is the case, this is a quick analysis in the light of Celtic-Buddhism. First of all, the family is about to have the celebration of Michael's wedding. The Old Peter now has the money and he is very pleased to have it. Bridget is also busy in arranging the house for the lady who is about to come. Patrick is happy for Delia will bring the dog with her. Even the priest is happy in this union. Suddenly, the Old Woman, as usual, a traveler, appears. When she appears, Michael is not happy, but custom prohibits him from keeping the Old Woman out of his home. Peter is reluctant to give the Old Woman some money, then he gives her some. Later on, she is given some milk, but no use. The demand is still higher. When the initiation by singing and poetry does its best in Michael, the Old Woman is ready to leave. Michael's initiation is now complete. Now he is ready to "give all to give [the Old Woman] all. To give [her] himself". Michael in this stage has no cravings, so does his father, Patrick and Delia. All are ready to give all. In this stage, Michael is ready to tread the eight fold path. Michael has no craving, and when one has no craving, he has no suffering. When craving stops, suffering stops. The eight fold path is awaiting for Michael who has got rid of all selfish longing and now is selfless. Michael is one person, but represents any Irish young man. When Michael has returned to the utmost selflessness, the whole nation is ready to give the same as Michael. As it had been hinted earlier, the sacrifice is a metaphorical union between Michael's soul and the nation's. This means the id stage. When the id (always needy) is ready to give, the national identity is in a good state. This means the ego has to go into battle and fulfill the id's desire for self-sacrifice.

The Old Woman returning young is a return to a previous stage of the symbol. Being a representative of the nation, this means a return to an age previous than this one; a return to the stage when the Irish were free. This seems a backward movement, but, as usual, it is a forward step, because the journey is psychological. It seems as there is a plot inside the plot. When the Old Woman comes into the house, she is directed to sit next to the fire. The fire place is where stories where told. Stories were and still are, a travel into the ancient past, where one can get a new meaning of an old tale. The Old Woman, being directed to the fireplace, is an indication to her in order to start telling her story especially when taking into consideration that tinkers were welcomed for this very reason; entertaining their host with their stories.

Again, as in <u>The Countess Cathleen</u>, "they have no need for prayers". This means the same; Celtic-Buddhism is their religion so there is no need to pray for them. They are in a higher degree than the person who prays for himself or for them. The Old Woman is here to foretell death, to connect the world of the living to the world of the dead. Those dead, also "shall be remembered for ever." This theme associates the two worlds too. Michael. Seeing that the martyrs are going to live forever in the nation's memory, decides to take arms as his predecessor; Cuchulain. The latter was told by a druid that the person who would take arms in that day, would be talked about all over the country, but his life would be short. Cuchulain goes to take his chance. The same is here told by the Old Woman, and the same is done by Michael. In the play, also, there are three generations. The Old Woman, Bridget and Delia. While the men we have Peter, Michael and Patrick. By leaving Delia at the eve of his wedding day and following the Old Woman, this supports the psychoanalysis of Michael being metaphorically engaged to his mother. The Old Woman, being the metaphorical mother of all especially when taking her as a goddess of fertility, makes Michael a complete Cuchulain. The latter also had two mothers. Moreover, Cuchulain, before he gets Emer; his wife, he goes to battle in order to prove himself suitable for her. Cuchulain's end is similar to the case of Michael's departure. Cuchulain was intrigued by many people and finally he is enchanted so he goes to fight the ghosts. The same trance is found on Michael's face when he is about to leave. As his predecessor's wife, Delia tries to stop him, but in vain. In Celtic myth, it was thought that some fairies were able to make somebody enchanted by touching his head. The Celts also held a high esteem for the power of word to the level of believing that a satirist could make the king's bone twist. By mingling the two myths, one can see that it is meant that the Old Woman has left the magical touch on Michael's head.

Leaving the myth for a while and taking a rest in history, it should be noted that the mentioning of milk and oat cake were the gifts by which the Irish peasants welcomed the French soldiers when they landed in Killala. Moreover, the commandant sent a letter to France reporting the simplicity these people were living in. Then, mentioning the "sheering of sheep" has some allusions to this historical fact. Another thing, the documented history mentions the joining of many peasants the French soldiers with "loys" as arms (Reamonn 4). During this rebellion, there was the Penal Law as one of the reasons which sparked this uprising. France looked upon the Catholic belief as something related to individual freedom and has nothing to say with policy. In Ireland, the Penal Laws were intended to be an eroding factor of Irish identity (5).

As it has been noted earlier, there are three successive generations in the play. As for women, it is meant to symbolize the past, present and future and at the same time to refer to the three goddesses. In Irish myth, it was thought that the triple goddesses were a symbol of strength. Moreover, the goddess of fertility has this triplet. Bridget herself has this feature:

"Taken together, the three women form a triple goddess. This triple aspect is one indication of Brigit's high status and her importance to the Celtic people, since the number three is usually linked to power and magic."(Matson 22). When she recommends that her son, Patrick should be a priest, it is an allusion to the fact that the church could not prevent the Irish from worshipping her, so they made her a saint. Later on, there was a saint who is named Bridgit. Even this saint's biography was much more about the pagan priest than about himself (22). Men, are used to refer to three generations only. Number three is also seen as lucky. The play being on the eve of a wedding, with the three generations celebrating this event, leaves no doubt that the real meaning is for national identity.

By interpreting the meaning of self-sacrifice, it can be seen as a call for the Irish to stop craving for money, and start to be selfless. In this way, all sufferings end. Michael, being a representative of any Irishman, returning to the id; the normally primitive and needy, to the level of being selfless, this means that the ego has to venture into the battlefield in order to satisfy the needs of the id. The id, in this situation, has become rebellious against the ego's suppression, and needs to express itself more freely. This theme can be clarified when Michael is about to leave behind the Old Woman. Firstly, he hesitates and then rushes away. This is the stage when his id has become completely selfless and in need to be unified with the mother figure at the same time. Therefore, all the Irish young men are selfless and in need to be unified with the mother figure; Ireland.

In this way, this time, the Irish are ready for a rebellious or military action in order to gain their freedom. It was seen in the previous play that Yeats called upon a peaceful protest. However, this time military action is the urge which he needs his country people to resort to. The id this time as in The Countess Cathleen, is selfless, but rebellious. The ego has to perform the id's desire by pouring blood as a kind of metaphorical marriage bond, for love of the mother figure; Ireland. This time, freedom is in the front and to achieve it self-sacrifice is the solution. Freedom is related to national identity and it is the ultimate aim of restoring this identity; the Abbey Theatre's influence on the Irish history was referred to earlier, and for this very reason these plays were performed.

Purgatory

This play focusses on the stage after death. In theosophy, when a person dies, his soul is put in a place where it is purified before it enters the soul world. Yeats, in his search for unity and national identity, saw the problem in front of this unity. It is the physical desires of the person that prohibits him from uniting with the world spirit. The term "purgatory" is also known in Catholic belief as a place where the soul is purified from its sins before entering into heaven. This belief was traced by Mary Sadlier and she finds out that this is almost a universal theme in addition to being found in Celtic myth (89).

The Old Man directs the Boy to look at the tree. Most likely, this tree is meant to symbolize the tree of wisdom. The three worlds, were thought to be linked together by this tree which is the source of all the wisdom in the world. It was also thought that trees held the spirits of the dead. This is illustrated before the very end when the Old Man compares the tree to a purified soul. Killing his father needs to be looked at as an Oedipus. However, killing his son should be looked as Cuchulain. All this will be studied in detail. Now it is better to take the general line of the play.

The play is about souls in purgation. These souls in this place are used to be looked at as being imprisoned in this place in order to be purified before going into heaven. The mother's and father's souls are in this place. However, the theme of the repeated action again and again is related to Theosophy. It is believed that if a person commits a crime, this crime is recorded in the memory of the space. Somebody with special talents could see the whole thing if he goes there. Moreover, the soul's crimes are thought to be hereditary as genetic heredity. In other words, an adulterous father begets an adulterous child and the cycle goes on. That is why, according the Old Man, he should kill his son; the mistake should be finished by killing the members in the cycle. The day of murdering the Boy is the anniversary day of killing the father, the day when the Old Man was sixteen years old, the day in which he was born and the day in which the house was burnt in addition to being the day in which the Boy is now sixteen years old. In this day, there was: a wedding, birth, death, burning of a house, and two murders. This is the cycle which always will repeat itself. Between the mother's death and the father's murder is sixteen years. When the Old Man killed his son, the Boy was sixteen years. This means the same cycle is repeated day by day and event by event, except that the murderer is the same. Therefore, the Old Man, as he declares, murdered his son in order not to get married, and beget an illegal child, as it seems from the context, and repeat the pollution of the race. In this way, one can see the cycle recurring over and over. To clarify the whole image, one has to resort to Celtic myth. In Celtic myth, it was believed that a dead body can be pacified by pouring a new blood over the dead person. The Old Man poured the father's and the son's blood over the mother's soul in order to pacify it. However, there is now two souls in need of pacification. Therefore, he has to commit more crimes in order to finish the torture of the already dead parents and child. As it is always the symbolism, mother is Ireland. Therefore, Yeats calls for more sacrifices in order to pacify the dead souls for Ireland and to satisfy the land itself. The mother, being dead for more than fifty years, returns young as the stage directions reveal. This means that the new blood has revived her. The horse being an active role player in this play is due to the fact that horses are usually associated with second-sight; a dead person being seen again as in Synge's <u>Riders</u>. Being the day of her wedding day, the day of her death and giving birth, means that the problem is in the marriage. The nation is associated to Britain and this association is illegal. Burning the house in the day of giving her birth means the marriage was destructive. That is why when the anniversary day of the wedding came, there was death, murder and destruction. However, there was born an Oedipus and a Cuchulain. Oedipus in order to kill the father; Britain and Cuchulain in order to kill his son. He is an Oedipus because, most importantly, he kills his father and he is a traveler. Moreover, in Psychoanalysis, he kills his father for the sake of his mother. As for being a Cuchulain, he is born by a woman and brought up by another in addition to being the murderer of his son who is begotten by a lovemaking relationship as his predecessor. Therefore, he is the person who will liberate Ireland and the mythical figure who will defend it against any invaders, the person who is ready to sacrifice his own son and father for the sake of Ireland. This person is ready to finish his own life for the sake of his mother/

Ireland as he was ready to kill the father and son. This can be clarified in the fact that he tries to relive the cycle and kill his father before he marries his mother. Or in other words, the thing is in memory. The nation is still occupied by memory. Therefore, the whole play can be regarded as being about national identity. What prohibits the nation's soul from being connected with the Life Spirit is her memory of being associated to an unlawful husband/ authority. National identity is dead while real independence has been achieved since sixteen years. Therefore, new sacrifices are needed in order to keep national identity. The Old Man is learned from the books and the whole library in his parent's house. But the Boy has no education. The Old Man wanted to preserve the house, but the Boy is happy for his grandfather getting the money and the house. Burning a library and a house in addition to the tree of wisdom being thunder bolted, leave little doubt that the play is about nation identity. Moreover, it is about the erosion of national identity and the reasons for this erosion. What is left of this identity is the memory of the sacrificed men for the sake of this mother. When looking into the Old Man's speech about old books, modern ones, noble classes and a royal heritage, in addition to the reference to his mother's high class, one can feel the Old Man as someone who is afraid over national identity. He is afraid over the noble race and that is why he kills his son (in addition to previously mentioned reasons). He regrets the burning of books, the destruction of the monuments of a high class by burning the house. He mentions the tree with a kind of resentfulness over its loss. Therefore, one can see that the tree itself is a complete image of national identity. It is about politics too. The Old Man says that the tree was beautiful and green before "fifty years". The play was written in 1939. By a small calculation, one finds the year 1889. It is the year when Parnell's affair made a split in Ireland's politics. Or more specifically, it is the last year of Parnell's leadership (Farry 134). The Boy is sixteen years old. He is negligible of national identity and should be assassinated. He is born, then, symbolically speaking, in 1923; the day of Ireland's division. That is why a Cuchulain and an Oedipus are needed; one to kill the father and the other to kill the illegitimate son or to unite the country as Cuchulain defended Ireland before. However, the son is not national. He cares for money and power not for the suffering mother. While the Old Man cares for the mother. Truly, destroying a house where parliament members and elite people came is a national crime. National identity is a treasure which needs more sacrifices in order to preserve it.

What is astonishing in this play is the repetition of the action every year; the mother's and the father's faults. This is found in Theosophy. It means that the souls have erred, and since there is no forgiving, one has to repeat his actions. Moreover, even in Theosophy, this theme is restricted to those who commit suicide. Therefore, Yeats considers these crimes as a kind of suicide. This means that the mother, in her marriage to the father, and the father being drunk, committed suicide. However, the mother died while giving birth to the child and the father died by his son's hands. This means that the mother, being willing to have a sexual affair and her readiness to beget, has polluted/ debased her status as a woman who has never set the bed for any. This again strengthens the theme of national identity. As for the child killing his father, it is as a retribution for debasing his mother and burning the house. It is a crime for cleansing the national identity. The child or Boy is also sacrificed for the peacefulness of the mother and in order not add to the debasement of national identity. The mother's soul, being sinful, (due to her attachment) could not unite with the Life Spirit. Therefore, the son killed the father to pacify her soul and to free her in order to be able to be united with the Life Spirit. This crime did not avail the mother, so he adds another. Every year, the mother returns to the stage when she was young, and commits her fault again. The national identity is imprisoned and cannot free itself due its crime. This crime is the treaty and the child is the illegitimate ruler assigned by the British. The first child begets a son of his own, who is the same by an illegitimate relationship. Therefore, national identity can return a young beautiful woman whenever the treaty is rejected and never celebrated as a day of independence again. This theme can be seen by the allusion to the day of the birth and death in addition to the wedding day being at the same day. To stop the cycle of the tormented souls, one has to return to the state when the wedding day was celebrated and stop the ceremony. This is what the Old Man is trying to do, but in vain because the wedding day is still celebrated in Ireland. More specifically, it might be that the engaged woman is Northern Ireland which is related to Britain.

In Celtic myth, the souls love certain places and go to these places when they are dead. This time, the souls love the house. This means he has an historical and mythical importance; a monument of national identity. It is the house of the Irish Parliament. The woman is Ireland since she owns the house and the husband is Britain. The Boy is the outcome of the treaty.

>
> Old Man. Re-live
>
> Their transgressions, and that not once
>
> But many times; they know at last
>
> The consequence of those transgressions
>
> Whether upon others or upon themselves;
>
> Upon others, others may bring help,
>
> For when the consequence is at an end
>
> The dream must end; if upon themselves,

There is no help but in themselves

And in the mercy of God.

This is a Buddhist belief. If the transgression upon others, others may bring help. If it is upon themselves, they have to help themselves. This again is a sign that the crimes or transgressions are suicide. For suicide is a kind of transgression against the self. The acceptance of the treaty is a transgression upon Ireland. That is why Ireland's soul or national identity is not unified and has to suffer. The solution Yeats poses is the rejection of the treaty and all its outcomes. In this way, the national identity can be freed from her purgatory. When there is no anniversary day of the wedding, the cycle will be broken. This cycle can be stopped by divorce. Divorce is the rejection of any kind of attachment to Britain; by rejecting the treaty. The assassination of the Boy is meant to symbolize the assassination of the relationship between the British and the Irish in order to free the mother's soul. The mother's soul, being in purgatory; a place between heaven and earth, symbolizes the imprisonment of national identity due its attachment to the British. In Theosophy, it is believed that the soul and spirit go to purgatory in order to free the soul from the spirit. During this process, the soul feels the desire to fulfill its desires, but being deprived of the physical organs assigned for fulfilling this desire, the soul begins to consume the feeling of desire until it consumes all desires. In this stage, the spirit releases the soul and the latter enters the soul world. Yeats alludes to the treaty as being the spirit which connects the soul to the body according to Theosophy. The spirit, being the father, is lustful and desiring in addition to being destructive of the soul by consuming too much drink. He also burns the library and is sexually aroused. He is a heap of desires and the soul has to suffer too much due to this spirit. As long as the spirit is attached to the soul, the soul will keep suffering and cannot enter heaven. Therefore, the soul/ national identity/ Ireland has to be released from the spirit/ treaty/ wedding day. In this meaning, one can look at the whole play as a regret over the imprisonment of national identity and the erosion of it in Ireland after the treaty, and the salvation of this soul by rejecting the treaty. If one goes deeper, one can see images of many people inside the play. One of the persons in the play is Parnell, and others such as parliament members.

"In Hugh Hunt's words, 'Ireland's national theater was born of a short-lived marriage between political and cultural nationalism in the form of the Celtic. . . Revival'(Hirsch 11). In the light of this quotation, one can see a new meaning of the marriage in the play. Political and cultural nationalism one represents the soul (cultural) and one for spirit (political). The marriage between political and cultural nationalism took place during Parnell's years. The son of this marriage is Parnell. Parnell, was about to make Home Rule in the year 1890 when his party divided. This year, as it is seen before, is mentioned by Yeats in an indirect way. The spirit and the soul, one for political and the other for cultural nationalism, means that cultural nationalism cannot be freed from its place in purgation until the political left frees it. This means that Ireland has to achieve its independence in political affairs. It also might mean that Cultural nationalism has to be separated from politics. However, most of the famous figures in Irish history associated cultural and political nationalism, which leaves little doubt that the intended meaning is the independence of the political decisions. This independence of the political decision, in order to free cultural nationalism, can be achieved by rejecting the treaty. More specifically, the downfall of Parnell is in 1889 (the year mentioned by the Old Man). The Boy is born in 1923 (the year of achieving Home Rule). This means, exactly, that Stewart Parnell was concerned over cultural nationalism, but the new leaders after the achievement of Home Rule are neglectful of cultural nationalism, and if Parnell was alive, he would have assassinated them in order to preserve cultural nationalism. Parnell's way is good, but the real Home Rule is not though Parnell campaigned for Home Rule.

The general argument becomes as follows. Parnell is the metaphorical father of the Irish policy. He is good and his way of combining political and cultural nationalism is good too. From the marriage between cultural and political nationalism, was born Yeats, who preserved cultural nationalism. When Yeats had become an "Old Man", a new generation of politicians, who polluted cultural nationalism and exploited its achievements on the political level, neglected it. Yeats, in this play, is claiming his role in achieving the independence, and comparing himself to Parnell. The Old Man is Parnell and Yeats at the same time. Parnell combined politics and cultural nationalism, but failed. Then, came Yeats with cultural nationalism and succeeded in what he considers Parnell had failed to achieve; Home Rule (by initiating revolutions as a reaction to his plays). Next, came the leaders of Home Rule, who neglected cultural nationalism. Yeats wants to assassinate them for the sake of Ireland; they do not care about Ireland's national identity. Therefore, there are three successive stages of Ireland's history in this play. "Yeats's three periods of modern Irish history are dramatized in the characters" (Torchiana 360). Purgatory is "…a drama-as-history lesson about the breakup of the Anglo-Irish heritage in Yeats's native land" (Rollins 45). Another supporting quote for the above analysis; "The Old Man…whose father… destroyed the last vestige of that Protestant past in denying Parnell" (Torchiana 360). Views and analysis differ, but what all are agreed about is that there are three stages of Irish history represented in this play. However, some say that these stages are from the French revolution to Parnell. This might be correct, but personally, I think that the similarities are with the modern history. Namely, from Parnell, passing with Yeats and finishing with Home Rule. More specifically, about the succession of the overwhelming interest of the Irish. Firstly political and cultural nationalism, then, from this marriage came Celtic Revival, and then Home Rule with indifference to cultural nationalism or national identity. What substantiates this argument is the association of allusions to politics with allusions to cultural nationalism and most importantly, to the combination of the two to mean political and cultural nationalism. These hints can be seen in the burning of the house where parliament members came to live, the burning of a library, the imprisoned soul, the mother figure who returns young every year, the tree, which becomes glistened with light after the assassination of the Boy, (representative of a neglecting person of national identity). This can be substantiated by Yeats' words about the play: " [I]n my play a spirit suffers because of its share, when alive, in the destruction of an honored house. That destruction is taking place all over Ireland **today**." (Barnet 993 emphasis). This means that the destruction is cultural, and the historical stages are modern. That is true, Mr. Yeats, thinkers lead tinkers and not the reverse.

In this meaning, one can add a last thing. Since the whole play is about who leads who, or the place of cultural nationalism in Ireland, Yeats mentions that the marriage was a degradation to the lady. This can be read as an allusion to the relationship between cultural nationalism and politics. Yeats sees that cultural nationalism was enchanted by the looks of politicians, but they degraded Ireland by degrading cultural nationalism. How this degradation happened, according to Yeats, is by neglecting the past, by degrading it, and debasing this cultural heritage. How specifically, this can be known by looking deeper into the Irish history. When the Gaelic League was taken by the

Republican Brotherhood, (Schulze 20) politics led cultural nationalism. When Home Rule took place, the politicians again took the stage instead of the plays. Every time, then, politics fails and cultural nationalism succeeds. Politics reaps what cultural nationalism sows. Every time, politics murders cultural nationalism. This time, Yeats wants the reverse to be the case in Ireland. He wants cultural nationalism to rule political nationalism. In this way, Yeats can rule Ireland's independence completely. Sure, he means that cultural nationalism is under the influence of politics. It might be that the man saw a kind of censorship over the thinkers' pens in Ireland, and wants the case to be reversed; thinkers' pens draw the politician's way not the other way.

Politics is, again, as the sticking spirit to the dead soul. Therefore, national identity has to free itself from politics. This confirms the two previously mentioned themes: Yeats is regretting the erosion of cultural nationalism and the influence of politics over national identity.

In psychoanalysis, the murder of the father leaves little doubt that the Old Man has returned to the id stage. Especially when taking into consideration that the Old Man mentions this plainly. He murders his father for the sake of his mother. The same can be said about murdering the Boy. By murdering the Boy, he means to assassinate the father a second time. The Boy is his grandfather, who has returned to the world in what is known as metempsychosis. This can be illustrated by referring to the reason the Old Man gives for his murdering of his own son; in order not to enchant another woman and sacrilege cultural nationalism. Another fact is the Boy's agreement about what his grandfather did; he got the house and the money. When the Old Man was busy in his contemplations, the Boy sneaks with the money. Another hint is the tree and the association of the horse's hoof beats with the time when the Boy is murdered. The tree for the Boy is an old man, but when the Boy is murdered, it becomes gleaned with light. Cultural nationalism is purified by murdering somebody whom the father was reincarnated in. the horse's hoof beats refer to the continuous anniversary debasement of the figure of the mother even though the father's reincarnation was murdered. Every time there is marriage between cultural nationalism and political nationalism, there will be hoof beats and cultural nationalism is not freed completely. What is correct, then, is the marriage between the mother figure/ Ireland and cultural nationalism/ Old Man. In this way, the nation can return into the id stage, and the mother's soul will be liberated.

The language of the play is poetic with some exceptions, but most of the time the language takes the form of iambic tetrameter.

>Old Man. Stop!

>Sit there upon that stone.

>That is the house where I was born.

Boy. The big old house that was burnt down?

………………………………………………

Old Man. But he killed the house; to kill a house

Where great men grew up, married, died,

I here declare a capital offence.

Boy. My God, but you had luck! Grand clothes,

And maybe a grand horse to ride.

This is the language which Yeats preferred in the theatre; a language to be chanted and sang and not spoken. By this way, he preserves two important features in the Celtic culture; their love of poetry and oral speech. In addition, poetry and poets were looked at as very effective in Celtic culture. Moreover, the Celts' love for story telling is preserved in this way. For the tales were told in verse and memorized in the same form. In this way, he can give the play a Celtic atmosphere; poetic language rehearsed in this form of speech, the audience lives the story as it occurs on the stage. It is a continuous tale. The subject is a tale and when told forms a new tale and so on so forth. These features—in addition to the fact that the storyteller in the Celtic culture was permitted to add some details under the condition of keeping the main themes untouched— are dramatized in the play's language.

Finally, in the play one can find that the Old Man is a preserver of cultural nationalism, while the father and the son are uninterested in it. They belong to political nationalism, which profits from cultural nationalism. Political nationalism sticks to the soul and never lets it be unified with the world. What is recommended by Yeats is that there should be freedom for cultural nationalism from politics, and that politics should follow cultural nationalism. Moreover, he recommends that the treaty should be rejected in order to liberate the soul of national identity.

Riders to the Sea

Rider to the sea is a direct reference to tinkers in Celtic culture. Tinkers used to trade with the settled many objects and animals including horses. There are many reference to traders in the play. Firstly, the fair which Bartley is about to leave to in order to trade with his horses. Secondly, Maurya buys the boards form Connemara, Cathleen has to sell the pig if there is a price going, and the rope in addition to fishing and knitting tools. However, every aspect has its connotation(s). Firstly, the horses are referents to tinkers and second sight. The Celts believed that many people, after their death, were seen by living people. These sights are usually accompanied by horses. This theme was traced by scholars to the conclusion that horses were companions to the Celts especially the warriors, who were the most returning. Horses were also present in funerals and this is the real reason of the dead with the horses. Moreover, when warriors died, the Celts believed that there is some kind of connection between the warrior's soul and his horse. When Cuchulain dies, the horses run away (Rolleston 200). Cuchulain was forbidden to eat the flesh of his namesake; a dog. The same for the riders, it is unlucky to eat from the horse's flesh literally or metaphorically. That was related to the first part of the title; Riders. The riders being riding into the sea refers to the fairies who ride the wind over the sea, touching or even looking for the dead souls over the sea. However, the complete title gives the impression of sailing on a ship. Therefore, one has the horses with their connotation of second sight and the image of spirits or fairies roaming the sea searching for the dead, in addition to the image of wind in the title itself. This gives the whole picture in mind to ghostly riders. What is left in the title is the fact that riders are warriors, but this time against the sea. Sea has nothing to be feared except when the wind blows. This means what is to be feared for Synge is the fairies who ride this wind. Therefore, the whole picture becomes a kind of a battle between the world of the dead and the world of the living. This is the main incident in the play; how Michael took Bartley into the world of the dead. Before going into this main theme, it is better to continue interpreting the meanings of other objects. The fishing net is something related to weaving. Weaving and spinning wheels are symbolic in Celtic myth. They refer to women who are associated with magic and fairy world. The boards are used for Bartley's coffin while they were bought for Michael. This refers to Michael being without coffin, and to associate the reason of Bartley's death to Michael. The nails are fairies repellents in Celtic myth. However, this belief was updated when Christianity came into Ireland. Before Christianity, any metal object was thought to be a fairies repellent. When Christianity prevailed, the belief became that any symbol of Christian belief is a fairies repellent. Therefore, Synge expelled Christianity and welcomed fairies by excluding the nails from Bartley's coffin. The pig with the black feet is also another symbol of death. Moreover, many myths mention the pig as being a companion of some goddesses, or magical pigs which were eaten up by warriors to refresh their strength, the historical implication of the pig as being excluded from exported animals during the Famine, the historical fact that the Irish lived by the price of pigs being fattened in the peasants' homes during the Famine, and the mythical-historical theme about animals in general killing people during the Famine and the mythical belief of the pig being a corpses eater. The stockings are knitted with "three" knots on them. Number three is used in Celtic myth for the belief in being lucky. The knife is also a fairies repellent in addition to being bought by a travelling salesman. As hinted, tinkers sold many objects and were looked at as excellent metalworkers and their goods were cheaper than the objects manufactured by settled people. The bread was done for Bartley, but eaten by his grave diggers. He is a distributer of death in the symbol of life and Christian symbol of Christ's flesh. Synge is known of subverting the Christian belief when talking about this belief. In this case, he means that Bartley's death will spread death in the symbol of life. Moreover, since bread is a symbol of Christ's flesh, Bartley does not eat it, but the grave diggers are expected to do. This is done in order to subvert the symbolic meaning of bread and distance Christening Bartley while associating Bartley with the grave diggers. In this way, the grave diggers are already digging their own graves by eating somebody's property and being associated with the world of the dead being grave diggers. It was thought that a dead one's property is still his own and it is unlucky to touch it. By eating the bread, the grave diggers have come closer to

Bartley's world. There are many interpretations for this event, but this is sufficient for the time being.

The main incident of the play is about a rider and his brother. Bartley was alive when he was seen by his mother riding while his brother Michael was dead but riding behind him. To make a clear division between Celtic myth and Celtic belief is somehow difficult. Therefore, both will be taken as myths. In Celtic myth, it was believed that the dead returned in certain days in order to take a living person into the world of the dead. They also believed in reincarnation, metempsychosis, and some traces of Celtic-Buddhism. In this play, the three are used. Firstly, when Bartley was a child, his brother was brought into the house. It was believed that a child should not be taken to funerals because it is unlucky. In Celtic-Buddhism, the soul returns to relive this life once again but in another body. The destiny of the previous soul determines much about the second's. This is well established. If not in religious books—due to the secrecy in dealing with them— in literature: Yeats' <u>Purgatory</u> and Ibsen's <u>Ghosts</u>. Moreover, it was believed that taking someone's property is unlucky even though he is dead. Bartley wears his brother's shirt, and the rope. The two objects are related to death. When Bartley dies, he is brought to the same place where his brother was brought to when he was a baby on his mother's lap. That is why when Bartley was brought dead Maurya indicates that the sea has nothing else to harm her. She knows how the cycle of destiny weaves diverse people's destinies at the same time like the fishing net or the spinning wheel. The spinning wheel contributes to the action. When the action accelerates, the spinning accelerates. The door opens every time there is death or mentioning of someone dead. It is due to the Celtic belief in the fairies and spirits riding the wind. When Bartley was brought into the house, Maurya was busy reporting what happened earlier. The tale is acted in front of the audience while being told. This is a Celtic custom in storytelling. Every storyteller was permitted to add some details but he had to keep the original story untouched. Moreover, the Celts believed that when one tells the story, he brings the characters into life again. In this way, one can add that the play mentions the theme of self-sacrifice. When Bartley leaves, he risks his own life in order to save the lives of the women. This can be traced back to the mythical belief that Cessair settled in Ireland after refusing to embark Noah's ark, in Ireland with fifty women and three men. While attending their duty to these women, two die out of exhaustion and the last runs away and hides. In <u>Riders</u>, the absence of men is analogous to the myth. In another myth, there are goddesses who were triple goddesses; the same one but has two other assistants. In addition to this, Maurya is associated with the world of druidism. In Celtic myth, some people were gifted to see their own destiny and others', those who were usually able of seeing second sights. All the dead and living are Maurya's relatives. This means that Synge meant the first settlement myth. Being a druidess, a goddess and woman, leaves little doubt that she is Cathleen Ni Houlihan. Being so, one has to look for the young face. This time, having two faces, one is younger than the other, means two sacrifices. This is what takes place during the play; one is found and the other dies in the action. As for the previous sacrifices, every sacrifice made the woman younger until the last one is mentioned as " a young girl" in the stage directions. Cathleen, however, is "twenty years old". This means that Nora is less than twenty. Moreover, one of the daughters is named "Cathleen". This means that Maurya has turned to be Cathleen due to the deaths for her sake, and now, due to Bartley's death, she has become Nora. This is supported by the fact that there is no given age for Nora, but can be figured as close to Cathleen's and less than twenty. Mei-Yen Chen speaks of a representation of three islands: "Geographically speaking, the Aran Islands form a small group of three, Irishmore, Inishmaan, and Inisheer…" (13). In this way, Synge represented real Ireland instead of a merely symbolic one. That is what is known about Synge; "one has to have realism and one has to have joy". Realistic setting and representation, and imaginary plot. Therefore, national identity is becoming younger every time a person dies on the island. Everybody leaves or hopes out of the island dies and the national identity becomes stronger. This leads to the interpretation of the play on Celtic-Buddhist grounds. All the dead people are sailors who were ambitious to see the world beyond their own land. While the men were craving for money and trade, the women suffered. When this craving ended, the suffering ended. In this way, the Old Woman can find peace in the final noble truth; the eight fold path. This time, she understood the rule; do not suffer by stopping to crave. She has to turn the glass upside down. Turning the glass is a gesture many scholars have pondered to look at. In fact it is a kind of resign to the Ultimate Power. The national identity now is ready to be unified with this power. Without this gesture and final words, national identity will have to suffer more. But being completely embracing of the Ultimate Power, she can be unified with this Spirit. Therefore, no more losses after this day. Any cup, turned up means the possibility of filling it again, but a turned upside down glass means the impossibility of filling it again. The glass is greed and desire when turned in this way, means the desire of no more desires. This can be clarified by associating the filling of the glass with funeral. Filling the glass means a new death, a new death is a new desire. When both end, the glass should be turned upside down. However, end of desire ends death. "No man can be living forever and we must be satisfied" is a resignation and resignation is to stop to crave. The general meaning goes to the heart of Celtic-Buddhist belief; the cessation of craving means the cessation of suffering.

In Riders, the action of the play is woven as a piece of clothes is woven by the spinning wheel. That is why such props are on the stage. First of all, there are white boards (referents to death), the fire, which does not extinguish (a referent to life) and the bread as a referent to life, but in Christianity. The spinning wheel is a device by which Synge weaves the incidents of the play.

[Nora comes in softly, and takes a bundle from under her shawl.]

Cathleen. [Spinning the wheel rapidly.]

What is it you have?

Nora. The young priest is after bringing them. It's a shirt and a plain stocking were got off a drowned man in Donegal.

The action is related to the spinning wheel very quickly in the play; when Nora brings the bundle, Cathleen spins rapidly. The relatedness of the priest is established in this short exchange too. Moreover, the priest is young, with no name to refer to him precisely. All this makes the priest as related directly to death, and has no power on the living. As for language, the use of "after" to refer to meaning normally conveyed by the present perfect tense is an Anglo-Irish syntactic rule. [The door which Nora half closed is blown open by a gust of wind.] every time there is a mentioning of the dead people, the door is related to the action, this can be clarified in reference to Celtic myth, where it was believed that the witches or fairies travelled by the wind (Monaghan 460).

Cathleen. There's a cake baking at the fire for a short space. [Throwing down the turf] and Bartley will want it when the tide turns if he goes to Connemara.

There is a relationship between the bread, as having a sacramental connotations and Bartley; the bread is for Bartley so he can eat it (related to life) when he goes in his travel.

Bartley returns for the rope, and in Irish myth, one should not return to take something he has forgotten; it is unlucky (Fleming107).

Cathleen. [Coming down.]

Give it to him, Nora; it's on a nail by the white boards. I hung it up this morning, for the pig with the black feet was eating it.

This is Cathleen's answer to Bartley's enquiry about the rope. The rope is hanged on a nail, the nail is related to death in Christian belief and more specifically, to crucifixion. The rope and the nail are close to the white boards, which in themselves reminders of death. Finally, the pig (believed to be an eater of corpses) with a "black feet" which is related to death in itself. Hanging the rope on the nail is to protect the rope from being eaten by the pig, is a kind of allusion to animal instinct, in discovering, or referring the relatedness of the rope of a dead body. Hindering the pig from eating the rope by hanging it on a thing related to Christianity, did not make the natural cycle of events to happen; the rope now is related to death, to Michael, to the pig and Bartley will use it for his ride. There is a reference here to the nail as participating in the weaving of Bartley's fate: Christian utensil related to death, transfers its power of being a reminder of the crucifixion into Bartley's destiny. Quickly, Maurya competes the weaving of all referents to death by asking Bartley to leave the rope because it will be needed to lower Michael's body down into the grave.

Bartley explains his need of the rope specifically to make it a halter in order to ride his horse. There is a realistic detail here, for Synge saw the islanders riding their horses without halters. When Maurya comes back, she reports what has happened near the well spring. First of all, comes Bartley riding his horse and Michael riding a grey pony behind him, with fine clothes and new shoes. They salute her and she could not return the salutation. The new shoes are related to Celtic myth, where it is believed the fairies wore new shoes, and shining clothes(Monaghan 520).The red pony, is most likely taken from Revelations, which tells of " 'a pale horse' ": " 'And I looked, and behind, a pale horse: and his name that sat on him was Death, and Hell followed with him.' " (qtd. In Grene 52). Horses were associated with a second sight due to their function in funerary ceremonies (Monaghan 250).

The fine clothes and new shoes are also might be related to Revelations, too; " 'and to her was granted that she should be arrayed in fine linen, clean and white.' " (52). Grene continues to see the failure of giving the bread is a "sacramental negation" (52). In other words, the interference of another Natural/supernatural force to prevent Bartley's baptism. For the distribution of bread is something related to Christ, Symbolizing His flesh. This idea will be needed later on. Not returning the blessing, or being unable to return it, is a sign of bad omen in Irish mythology (Fleming 107). Moreover, seeing Michael and Bartley in this situation, brings to the mind the Irish myth related to the dead as supposed, to return back to take the living and join them to the kingdom of the Dead(Fleming 107, Grene 53).

Kiberd suggests that Synge often, "when promoting an Irish pagan ideal, subverted Christian practices"(405)"…the absent or dead father, the death of the remaining son, and Maurya's vision of Michael riding the pony represent a subversion of the holy Trinity…"(Ritschel 105). When Maurya finishes her talk, Nora reminds the audience of priest's words that God would not leave Maurya without a son living, Maurya answers, that he does not know much about the sea. In other words, one has not respect the sea forces and not go on challenging them. The priest thinks that the death of Maurya's family is in God's hand, and God will not take all of the sons, especially if she prays all the night. However, Maurya sees it differently; she reads the weaving of one's destiny. That is why she says "for I won't live after them". She has read something related to her destiny being connected to the world of the dead. When Maurya tells the audience of her lost kinsmen, one can notice the similarities between one's death and the other's:

"There were Stephen, and Shawn, were lost in the great wind, and found after in the Bay of Gregory of the Golden Mouth, and carried up the two of them on the one plank, and in by that door." Both of them lost (1) then found (2) and brought on the same plank (3) by the same door (4).

"There was Sheamus and his father, and his own father again, were lost in a dark night, and not a stick or sign was seen of them when the sun went up."

Again, they were lost together, without anything related to one of them.

There was Patch after was drowned out of a curagh that turned over. I was sit-ting here with Bartley, and he a baby, lying on my two knees, and I seen two women, and three women, and four women coming in, and they crossing themselves, and not saying a word. I looked out then, and there were men coming after them, and they holding a thing in the half of a red sail, and water dripping out of it – it was a dry day, Nora – and leaving a track to the door.

Patch's destiny and Bartley's are tied together since Bartley had been a baby. Patch drowned when the "curagh" turned over, and Bartley was knocked down by the horse. This is what the Celts called the "fetch"; it is like a ghost or a shell that hovers in the surroundings. When one sees his exact image or in the graveyard, it is mostly death awaiting him. Those who see the fetch, see a second sight and can also see their own fetches (Monaghan 185).

Just in fear of confusing the reader, there will be no more themes here, but this last one. Those who died in violent ways are most likely to return to the world of the living and they can be sent away by holy water (Monaghan 228).

Speaking about two or three or even four women keening without speaking, men carrying a thing with a half of red sail and water dripping out of it is a kind of a new apparition/ vision, but this time it is about something will happen in the near future. In other words, it is history being recorded in the memory of time, and being replayed again. This quotation is almost the same as the stage directions which will not be quoted so that there will not too much confusion. Although the quotation here is similar to the stage directions, the movement of women narrated firstly by Maurya then by the stage direction, is separated from the movement of men carrying the body, leaving a little space for Maurya and her daughters to link the death of Patch, Michael and Bartley together. Maurya wonders if this is Patch's body, Cathleen says it is Michael's and handles his clothes to his mother. Cathleen asks if this Bartley's body, and one of the women confirms Cathleen's speculations to be true. This is related to the Irish myth, which indicates that the dead return back to the world of the living to claim them. Moreover, seeing Michael riding with his brother, is another indication of the same idea (Fleming 108, Grene 54). There is something related to prophecy in this incident; Maurya tells the audience of it before it happens on stage. Prophecy is something related to goddesses and even to normal women in Celtic mythology (Monaghan 300).

Maurya, as an expert in requirements of making a coffin, would not forget the nails, but Synge is alluding the convergence of Christianity with paganism in this small piece. As referents or symbols of Christ's crucifixion, they are excluded from the coffin. Christ died due to fixing nails into his body;

the nails are connected to Christianity, and being required to make a coffin, make the nails charged with heavy meanings in Christianity while they perform a normal role in paganism. Therefore, they must be excluded. The bread, which is supposedly intended for Bartley, now will be eaten by the grave diggers; it is related to death and not to the living from both sides: being intended to be Bartley's food, makes the bread related to the world of the dead from one hand, and being eaten by the grave diggers is another link of bread to the same realm of Bartley's. The failure to give Bartley the bread is a refusal of Christianity. Moreover, the absence of the nails is related to the absence of Christianity; nails are symbols of Christ's crucifixion, but they are related to Celtic myth in the same line, which is intended by Synge: in order to keep the fairies away, one has to puncture a nail in the dead body. Moreover, any Christian symbol was thought to be a fairies repellent (Monaghan 89). It is a double sided theme; fairies are more tolerated than Christianity and the absence of nails means that the fairies will come and interfere in the world of the living once again, but no for Christian interference. Therefore, it is somebody's destiny being woven from small pieces as small as the nails or even the meaning of forgetting the nails to somebody else's fate. The nails, having Christian and Celtic connotations are not the only double-charged symbols in Irish culture; Maurya holds Bartley's feet, puts Michael's clothes on Bartley's feet and then leaves the feet. In Celtic myth, it was firstly thought that one had to tie the dead person's feet in order to prevent him from disturbing the living. However, this belief was modified to indicate that it is better to leave the feet free in order to speed the person's travel into the world of the dead (Monaghan 390). Moreover, the distribution of the bread is something like weaving the grave diggers' destiny, and tying them to the world of the dead by the bread. The bread becomes a symbol of spreading death and not a symbol of life. For the men are going to eat the bread, they are going to eat Bartley's food. Maurya uses Michael's stick to walk, now her destiny has started to be woven and she comes closer to the world of the dead; it is unlucky to use someone's property even after he is dead. It is still his property. Bartley wears Michael's clothes, and soon he joins him. Maurya rakes the fire aimlessly until it is almost extinguished. It is thought that the fire is related to the prosperity of the house, and should not be extinguished, especially when there is somebody ill (Fleming 107). The girls are urged by Bartley to sell the pig with the black feet in order to eat. They are going to eat by selling a symbol of death. Moreover, this theme has a real background; the Irish, especially during the famine, had nothing to eat except selling a pig which they used to fatten in the house (Monaghan 100). The nets for fishing are other reminders of how destiny is weaved, the stitching, especially Nora's stitching of three knots on Michael's stockings are used to distinguish him from other sailors' destiny. In other words, the knots distinguished his fate in this way. They are the means by which his identity is confirmed. Also in the same line, number three is related to Celtic myth, and considered to be a lucky one (123).

That is why the three knots were responsible for distinguishing Michael's clothes.

The priest's declaration that God will not leave Maurya without any son living proves to be a kind of speculation, which comes to the opposite of its message. Being "young" refers to him being ignorant of the way of life on the island, and portrays him as not having any authority over the island or even a foreign person to the whole surroundings. His absence might be related to a historical fact, that one priest was responsible for more than one island, and he kept travelling from one to the other. However, the weather being too bad, this means that the priest is on the island, but he did not come to the funeral because he is not needed as the nails. They can manage without Christianity; for Maurya is now performing the supposed role of a priest. However, she is sprinkling a holy water on the clothes and the body. This holy water is not related to Christianity but to paganism. One must mention that when the mourner is a mother, she mentions the sufferings of birth (Kearney 130). Critics came to the conclusion that the turning of the glass upside down and the performance of papal authority, Maurya

performs the Catholic priestly rite of sprinkling Holy Water on the clothes of her drowned but unrecovered son', compounding the 'subliminal outrage' by 'mumming a scene from ultra-Protestant prophetic tradition' this irony is, itself, metatextually ironized when the Authorized Version of the Bible turns the tables on its own colonizing Protestant authority: the mimed passage warns of Jehovah's punishment of Jerusalem for corruption and injustice." (Richards 85).

The passage which warns of the punishment is to be found in the Old Testament reference (2 kings 21: 13) "And I will stretch upon Jerusalem the line of Samaria, and the plummet of the house of Ahab: and I will wipe Jerusalem as a man wipeth a dish, wiping it, and turning it upside down"(qtd.in. McCormack 192). One has to support this quotation by referring to a previous idea about Synge's subversion of the Christian practices when he is performing a pagan ideal.

The details of the story come from Synge's experience on the Aran Islands. The articles Bartley picks up before he heads off to the sea—Michael's shirt and his own purse and tobacco—are articles found on a man washed ashore in Donegal. For three days the people of the island tried to fix his identity, which was determined by his sister who pieced together all she could remember about his clothes, purse, his tobacco box, and stockings….his name was Michael, and she said "please God, give him a decent burial" (Fleming 109).

The theme of one's coffin to be lent or used to burry another person is also documented in Synge's Aran Islands, where a man gave up the boards which he was keeping for his alive but ill mother, to another woman who died out of typhus(Fleming 109).

The apparition which Maurya saw is also told by a woman, whose son was drowned, that she saw her son riding on a horse while the horses were herded to the boats. Another woman who was thought to be taken by the fairies, returned to tell the people that there were four hundred or more of the fairies were riding on horses, and she herself rode a gray horse behind them(Fleming 109).

The last line of the play comes from a letter addressed to Synge from one of his friends, the letter written in Irish, on February 1 1901"….it is a sad story to tell …we must be satisfied because nobody can be living forever." Synge's Riders was written later that year (Fleming 109).

Language of the play:

Nora. In a whisper to Cathleen.]

She's quiet now and easy; but

The day Michael was drowned you could hear her crying out

From this to the spring well.

It's fonder she was of Michael,

And would anyone have thought that?

Cathleen.

It's the same stuff, Nora; but if it is itself

Aren't there great rolls of?

It in the shops of Galway,

And isn't it many another man may

Have a shirt of it as well as Michael himself?

The language is poetic in prose, though less poetic than the Playboy. However, the tragic meaning must be conveyed in expense of the poetic style. Moreover, there is an Anglo-Irish syntax in the play. Examples are abundant but here are some:

Maurya. In the big world the old people [do be] leav[ing] things after them

for their sons and children, but in this place it is the young

men [do be] leav[ing] things behind for them that [do be] old.

The form [do+be] +verb+ing is an Anglo-Irish syntactic rule.

Cathleen…for his body is after being found…

This is the Anglo-Irish alternative of the present perfect tense in formal English.

It should be clear now but here is a final example

Cathleen. There's someone after crying out by the seashore.

Mauray…. I was sitting here with Bartley, and he a baby, lying on my two knees, and I seen two women, and three women, and four women coming in, and they crossing themselves, and not saying a word…

First of all, the use of "seen" is an Anglo-Irish style. Moreover, as it can be 'seen', the whole sentence is a succession of phrases without full stops. This, again, is an Anglo-Irish style especially after the verb 'seen'(Hickey 14).

In this play again, Synge tried to bring the national aspects on the stage; historical, mythical, and contempt for Christianity. Language is also used to highlight national aspects by using a national language; the Anglo-Irish style.

The Playboy of the Western World

Christopher Mahon is read: Christ of her home man. When he arrives, they welcome him because they are somehow pagan especially Pegeen. Also his killing of his father is read by them as an Oedipus, and due to their love of storytelling. Moreover, they are in complete contempt of Christianity, and he is less Christian than the other men, especially Shawn, they welcome him. Therefore, their welcome of Christy is based on their love of national identity aspects that are related to paganism: storytelling, love for the strange, love of courage, a kind of strike to the suppressor and hatred of Christianity. When Christy is living with them, he is using their own powerful means to be stronger, their poetry talk, sports and oral speech. With these things, he establishes himself as a master, especially when one remembers his new clothes. When the old Mahon returns, they discover that Christy is only a liar. Therefore, the story loses its effect on them and Christy is rejected for he is now like anyone of them: he did not kill his father, so he is a normal Christian person. Christy strikes his father for the second time. Now the small community tries to hang him basing their decision on Christian belief that they have to guard their property from being a place of committing crimes. They attempt to judge Christy's deed from the Christian point of view, and not noticing that they are going to hang Christ according to his own teachings, or a more strict belief than

Christ's himself. The old Mahon sees the foolishness of the Mayo people; when he asks them why they are doing so to Christy, they reply that they are applying a Christian doctrine of taking a complete guard over their property so that nobody commits a crime in it. He realizes that now things are done, and that the Irish people are now more Christian than Christ himself. At this moment, the old Mahon is reconciled with his son because now Christy, is better and more easy going than the people of Mayo, especially that his name is still 'the Playboy', a person indulged in entertaining himself in pleasures to the utmost level. Old Mahon now sees Christy as less religious than the people of Ireland. Therefore, he accepts to be enslaved by him: there is nobody left in Ireland who is not Christian. However, he is still not too religious as Shawn.

The people of Ireland has to be enslaved by the Playboy wherever he goes. Moreover, the religion is Christianity, old traditions are under control of this religion, literature is now Christian and every aspect of life is Christian and under the transformation from pagan into Christian. Pegeen is lamenting for Christ(y) so he is more moderate in his Christian belief than Shawn, and he can keep some traces of paganism in Ireland.

Christy introduced himself to the community on pagan terms. Therefore, he was loved by all. These aspects are: killing a father (throwing away the religious authority or overthrowing it in Mayo), the murder is a strike against a suppressor, so it is welcomed on pagan terms (as it is the case in Celtic literature), their love of story-telling, their love for the new.

He is theorized on pagan terms and not on Christian ones, otherwise, Shawn should be the playboy. His self-awareness is achieved by using the poetry talk and oral speech that the Irish are well-known of. His first coming is related to the idea of the noble tinker, who was displaced by the strangers, and whom the Irish race belongs to. This is seen when linking Christy with the poet O'Sullivan, in the marriage rites before Old Mahon appears; the tinkers are known of paying less attention to marriage rites (Burkes 30).

At the end, Christy and his father are going to go on travelling the whole country. Synge's message, then, Irish people are more Christian than Christ himself, and if Christ came to Ireland, they would hang him according to Christian beliefs that Christ tolerates. Synge says, then, avenge your national identity, but not on Christian principles, or you will end up more Christian than Christ. Try to recover your freedom by rejecting Christianity. For Ireland, being Christian, is what makes her enslaved by the British. In other words, if you cannot revolt against Christianity, do not be more religious than Christ. This makes Ireland enslaved and makes her national identity withdraw and erode.

Therefore, since Christy is the savior of the community by his moderate religious beliefs than most of Irish people, he is a real hero. He is going, at least to quench the highly strict religious beliefs in Ireland, and try to make the Irish increase their tolerance with religion. That is why he is called a playboy of the western world; although he is Christ himself, he is considered as a playboy in comparison to the too much religious Irish people. Thus, Christy overcame the community in their national identity aspects, and they overcame him in his own religion. That is why, again, he is named a playboy. The last message is, Pegeen (pagan Ireland) needs Christ(y) to make her less religious than actually she is. Therefore, Christy is now the only holder of pagan (purely Irish, purely national) aspects in the play. He is poet, a wanderer, tolerating about religion and above all, a playboy, which in itself holds the meaning of the least religious person in the western world, a sports man, and courageous. Pegeen is lamenting her loss of is the new hero of Ireland; a person who is hardly attached to religion, brave, a poet and a wanderer. If one is not speculating too much, this is Synge himself. He is Christ(y), who is wandering in Ireland in order to make her less Christian, i.e., trying to preserve its national identity. He is hardly a Christian, a wanderer (related to the notion of tinkers; the preservers of national identity), and a poet who has tales to tell.

Synge is indicating his indebtedness to Irish people who made him the most person who is worried about national identity, the person who found in Ireland his self-awareness, his Irishness. He is inviting the Irish to go on Ireland, like him, or like Christy, in order to be less Christian, to be poets, to learn oral speech, to be wanderers, and to love Pegeen (Pagan Ireland) as Christy did.

When he acknowledges that the words are taken from the mouths of the Irish people, he means that his language is realistic; the oral speech patterns with their pronunciation, idiom and syntax. Moreover, the play being about Irish peasants is something related directly to the national identity. For the peasant was seen as the real Irish man, his language is the closest to that of the Irish, or at least, distinguished from the Standard English. The play, containing old Mahon being enslaved by Christ(y) is another aspect of national identity, referring to enslavement of the Irish people; the occupation of Ireland by England.

The historical background of the play being about a man who has killed his father, is another national aspect. The notion found in the west of Ireland concerning the protection of a criminal is also national. Wandering, as referred earlier, is national, and the celebrated national aspect is language. Pegeen says at the end of the play that the last few days have taught her that there is a great gap between a gallous story and a dirty deed. Now the power of the Irish language (being oral and poetic), made a gallous story turn into being a dirty deed; the Irish peasants' poetic oral speech, made Christy a 'likely gaffer' or even the only playboy of the western world while he started as a shy, coward boy.

This is highly national; as if Synge is saying: If you want to be national, preserve this treasure represented by your ability to talk oral, poetic, Hiberno-English, keep in touch with the main sources of this language; peasants, be wanderers, be more tolerating in religion, and love your country.

On the other hand, he criticizes the Irish, seeing them as more religious than Christ himself. This idea can be seen clearly from the very beginning of the play when Shawn is asked to stay the night with Pegeen, he refuses and flies out of the house, leaving his coat in Michael's hands. Whereas it was thought that leaving one's wife with the guest as a kind of hospitability. Shawn always refers to the Pope, Father Reilly, and the fear of the Irish from this authority. For the same reason, maybe, he refuses to wear the woman's clothes, for he thinks that his clothes are referents to the label. Moreover, many myths mention the hero's escapement by disguising in a woman's clothes (Ebbutt 300).

The setting itself is national; a cottage in the remote countryside, where a traveler—normally referring to the tinker—comes to be served. In other words, the ideal Irish, represented by the tinker, or traveler, is visiting a peasant in a remote place, where one finds Pegeen (Pagan Ireland). Very quickly, Pegeen establishes the connection between the noble race, 'Solomon' or even directly referring to Christy as descending from a noble race, due to the same fact that the Irish, at the time Synge wrote his play or maybe earlier, came to the conclusion that the tinkers were a noble race who were displaced or overthrown from their respectable place, and kept wondering all over the country, and that the Irish race descends from this same race. Moreover, the Irish thought of the tinkers as first of all coming from the East, so that is why there are many referents to the east in the play: Pharaoh's ma, for example, is a direct reference to Egypt, where the Irish believe the Gypsies came from. Christy's reference to the Eastern world 'from here to the eastern world'.

Pegeen refers to herself being afraid of the tinkers living near her house. "Synge's work indicates that the terror of sexual assault by an unknown, male [o]ther is common to both sedentary and tinker women" (77 Burke). Synge here is dissolving the boundaries that separate the itinerant from the sedentary, which means the ultimate national aspect that one can think of. For the tinker is the exotic type of Irishness. "The tinker is the carrier of a Celtic or pre-Celtic authenticity...the embodiment of a kind of concentrated archaic Irishness" (Burke 45). On the other hand, the dissolving of the boundaries that cut the tinker from the sedentary, one will see Dubliners and tinkers are the same. Here one can refer to the fact that Christy is also a referent to Christ:

"Evocations of the nomadism of Jesus have been made by commentators and by peoples of the road themselves to explain their 'innate' urge to travel, although the motif was occasionally Hibernicized by inserting St Patrick into the role of Christ"(20 Burke).

Also the idea of the tinker is attached to the Famine. And lastly, some associate tinker's travel to the Jews, who were condemned for their role in the crucifixion (20).

> Pegeen. [Standing beside him, watching him with delight.] -- You should have had great people in your family, I'm thinking, with the little, small feet you have, and you with a kind of a quality name, the like of what you'd find on the great powers and potentates of France and Spain.

This is the Gypsy's work: to tell somebody about his past, in order to attract his attention, then to start foretelling his future. Foretelling or fortune telling is based on assumed reading of the palm (It is satirized here in reading the foot) and the meaning of the name. It is also associated with Celtic myth; poets, midwives, and druids were expected to prophesy (Monaghan 148).

Moreover, attaching Christy to the dynasty of French and Spanish kings is based on the assumption that the Tinkers first of all came to Ireland from Spain. The idea of the Tinker is also found in France, and as a political alley to Ireland, this made the Irish dramatists use the French style (Burke 99). 'Synge was 'one of the few Irish writers who Europeanized Ireland without degaelicizing it" (101).

Christy. [Getting his boots and putting them on.] -- If there's that terror of them, it'd be best, maybe, I went on wandering like Esau or Cain and Abel on the sides of Neifin or the Erris plain.

'Synge's antediluvian Ireland was both a return to the Old Testament…A strikingly Irish evangelical interpretation of Old Testament characters and Irish geography informs the playboy of the western world, in which Christy foresees himself 'wandering like Esau or Cain and Abel' on 'the Erris plain' (Burke 117).

> Philly. Supposing a man's digging spuds in that field with a long spade, and supposing he flings up the two halves of that skull, what'll be said then in the papers and the courts of law?

Jimmy. They'd say it was an old Dane, maybe, was drowned in the flood.

"The desperate eras of antediluvian epoch and the Viking encroachments fuse counter-chronologically: if unearthed, the skull of Christy's presumed victim would be understood as 'an old Dane, maybe, was drowned in the flood" (Burke 117). This refers to the Old Mahon as being a pagan. For he refused, or was denied to go on the Noah's ship. Moreover, Philly is reminding the audience of the dead people during Potato Famine. The link between finding the body and the digging for "spuds" makes one remember the Potato Famine.

There are other historical facts in the play. For example, Shawn offers Christy half a ticket to America, which refers to the immigration of the Irish to

America during the Potato Famine "Due to a devastating potato blight in the years 1845 to 1852 the population of Ireland decreased from 8.2 million to 6.5 million people. 10 percent of the population died, another 10 percent emigrated...mostly to America" (Schulze 19). The word "shift" is also linked with the idea of Potato Famine which will be stated later. However, one can say that the word first was spoken by Pegeen to insult Widow Quin in the context which means exactly that the Widow Quin cannot afford to buy a white shift since the Flood dried. The same word is used later by Widow Quin imagining herself stitching a shift. These two uses of the word are meant to shock the audience by making Christy use it; he represents the British, and a word linked to Famine which most Irish people consider as done by the British intentionally.

> Pegeen. And myself, a girl, was tempted often to go sailing the seas till I'd marry a Jew-man

Here the reference to the hatred of Christianity is clear; the Jews participated in the crucifixion of Jesus and some believe 'that St. Patrick cursed tinkers to wander because a tinker tradesman drove the nails that pierced Jesus'' and because a tinker 'attempted to trick him out of gold' (Burke 21). Pegeen, the real pagan Ireland, Noah's kinswoman, was often tempted to go on sailing to find a person who descends from the same dynasty that crucified Jesus. This is the utmost betrayal of Jesus due to hatred. Ironically, Pegeen is about to marry Christ(y). A lady, who always wanted to go on wandering till she would find the person who crucified Jesus, is ready to marry Christ(y) to avoid being married to an Irish man due to his complete devotion to Christianity.

Pegeen rejects Christy because he is a liar, so he murders his father to prove his truthfulness. Again, Pegeen rejects him. This can be read in the light of the often-quoted Pegeen's words: "there is a great gap between a gallous story and a dirty deed"

A gallous story is meant to imply literature, or oral culture and a dirty deed is meant to imply reality: for the action of the gallous story is the same dirty deed. In other words, this is realism versus reality. Pegeen rejects romanticism, therefore, Christy leaps to realism thinking this will satisfy Pegeen. Pegeen again rejects realism by torturing Christy. And now this is the meaning of the above quotation: there is a great gap between realism and romanticism, and Pegeen is in this gap that separates realism and romanticism. That is why she rejects both. Synge, here is telling the audience that this Ireland, enslaved culturally by being thrown in the gap between her being occupied and her glorious past. Moreover, the transformation of the lie into romanticism, and then the transformation of romanticism into realism means transforming the glorious past, bit by bit into a glorious present.

Shawn comes close to Pegeen and speaks to her about being ready now to be wedded. She 'hit[s] him a box on the ear. -- Quit my sight. (Putting her shawl over her head and breaking out into wild lamentations.) Oh my grief, I've lost him surely. I've lost the only Play-boy of the Western World.'

Hitting Shawn a box on the ear is related to 'Cessair, The book of Invasions details the settling of Ireland before the Flood by Cessair, a figure referred to as Noah's kinswoman' (Burke 117).

Pegeen's final rejection of Shawn Keogh, portrayed by Pegeen boxing his ear, curiously echoes the medieval mystery play Noah's Flood, from the Chester cycle...since she vehemently opposes Noah's efforts to follow God's commands, she emerges as one of the period's fist independently minded women (of literature). Given that the play (in its historical context) promotes Christianity, with Noah's wife as the main obstruction to God's plan, she arguably represents paganism, especially as she boxes the ears of the devout Noah...Pegeen as Synge's pagan mirrors Noah's wife in this instance as she strikes the obsessively devout Shawn" (Ritschel 97, 8).

Making the rejection of Shawn clear in its reference to the refusal of Christianity by Pegeen (pagan Ireland), now it is sure Pegeen will lament Christy. Here Synge is satirizing Shawn; he is more devoted to Christianity than Christ himself. Pegeen's lament also means that now she has faced reality and seen her represented by the normal religious Shawn, tries to cling to romanticism represented by Christy. Therefore, Christ(y) is mirrored as the least religiously devoted person in Ireland, who suits Pegeen for being less religious and suitable in age too.

Romanticism is linked to paganism while realism is attached to Christianity. Here one could say that Ireland is stuck between pagan and Christian beliefs, represented by Pegeen. Moreover, she is bewildered by two choices, one is Christ himself and a Christian Irish man and the latter is more devoted to Christianity than the former.

Back to the general line of the play, one can find that Pegeen welcomes Christy after he tells his story. Then being discovered, she rejects him. Being rejected, he bring words into deeds. Seeing the truth, she rejects and torments him. This can be rephrased as romanticism versus realism. Pegeen, by refusing romanticism, she embraces realism. Christy transforms romanticism into realism so that he can impress Pegeen. While she tells Christy that she has discovered the gap between romanticism and realism, she is unaware that she has fallen in the same gap/ hole herself has discovered. Rejecting romanticism makes her come into realism and rejecting realism makes her go back into romanticism. Christy leaves, then Pegeen laments, this means that she has come out of the gap that separates realism and romanticism and decided to be romantic; pagan as much as possible. Now she can make the distorted look beautiful, the normal as unusual, and the natural as supernatural.

> Christy. Ten thousand blessings upon all that's here, for you've turned me a likely gaffer in the end of all, the way I'll go romancing through a romping lifetime from this hour to the dawning of the judgment day.

Christy is indicating his intention to go on telling his story; i.e., Christianity. He refers to the Judgment Day as the final day of telling the story, which leaves little doubt that he is Christ. The most pagan woman/lady in Ireland, is lamenting the loss of the—supposedly— most devoted person to Christianity. She has no choice other than this. For Shawn is a normal Irish man, but he is more devoted to the church than Christ. Shawn represents any Irish man. The evidence, though may look strange, but hints to this: Christopher Mahon can be read as Christ of her Man. When one goes further and rearranges the letters, he can find that it becomes Christ of her Ho(me) man.

The heavily quoted word 'shift' to justify the riots, is used by Christy. However, even Synge borrowed it from the British, who were referring to the Irish woman's underwear item: 'W. J. McCormack theorizes that Synge was influenced towards using "shift" by a missionary's report on the horrific effects of the 1840s Famine in west Ireland: none of either married or unmarried women can affords more than one shift"(Ritschel 98). Therefore, Christy is Christ but he goes to adapt a pagan way of life compared to Shawn. He is going to spread Christianity, but at the same time he is going romancing. This can be linked to the general line of argument that Synge is telling the Irish that they are too religiously devoted, to the level of being religious more than Christ. Even Christ is going to live a romanticized life, but Shawn cannot be other than a church devout. Pegeen is lamenting for Christ himself, as the last romantic person in the whole of Ireland. This brings one face to face with the fact that the Irish, though took Christianity from Britain, became more religiously devoted/extremely religious than the British themselves. Synge here alludes to the Irish that if you are followers of Christ, follow his way of life and go on romancing, by being less religious and by making a gallous story of the least action. This will make you able to bring the gallous story into being a dirty deed. The dirty deed is realistic, now reject the dirtiness in the deed or the deed itself and it will turn into romanticism again.

This is how a nation builds a new national identity: small achievements by normal people, are romanticized to be gallous stories. These gallous stories have heroes, now those heroes are able to act their previously written plots or even plays (most of the time the story takes the form of a play especially in oral cultures) to make the stories become history. This history now can be romanticized. This romanticism of history makes a new national identity.

Here one can figure out Synge's most genuine ideas; this is my play, it is romanticism. Now you audience reject it, (they did) and now I made my play come into fact. I made a revolution out of romanticism. This argument can be validated by referring to a letter from Synge to his fiancée after the riots "now we will be talked about…we will be remembered in the history of the Irish stage" (Schulze 67). Now this revolution is going to live in the next generations' memory, and being romanticized. Although he did make a revolution in the Abbey, maybe he was intending of his play to be internalized—after being comprehended—and acted in real theatre; actual Irish life. Therefore, he intends to say: Be Christian, though it is bad, but be less devoted to your religion than Christ, so that you can go on romanticizing. Since Pegeen loves those who are romantic, who are not too devoted to Christianity. If the audiences revolt against Christy, they are revolting against Christ, (he is not devoted enough to Christianity) against Synge (he is romantic) and against the British (they are not romantic. They are enslaving the Irish). If they are revolting against Shawn, they are revolting against themselves. So now Synge leaves the audience in these three choices: revolt against Christ or against the British or against Synge. They decide to revolt against Synge. Now Synge is romantic. Therefore, the riots made him realistic. Synge says in the introduction that one has to be realistic and romantic. The revolution against Christ is to stop being too religious or even to abandon Christianity. Revolting against Christ because he is romantic makes the Irish more realistic than Christ. Now again realism and romanticism go hand in hand in Ireland. Revolting against Christy as a representative of the British is realistic. At the same time he is romantic. Therefore, revolting against the British is realistic, but they should not revolt against the romantic to make it realistic. Now when the audience revolted against Synge's play, they revolted against the thing Synge was warning them (ironically, he is leading them into) the gap that Pegeen has fallen in. Pegeen laments Christy, she then laments freedom and paganism by lamenting over the loss of Christ(y). Therefore, there is nothing left to revolt against except the enslavement of the Irish and the religious devotion in the Irish, to find that Christy is a national hero once again.

Synge's message here is: do not revolt against the romantic, for you are making it realistic and making yourselves realistic by revolting against the romantic. However, revolt against the realistic to make it romantic: revolt against Christianity and occupation to make them romantic; Ireland will be less religious, and consequently more pagan, and be free; i.e., romantic too.

What adds to the ambiguity of this play is that the riots are intended by Synge to contribute to the meaning of the play. If the audience is revolting against the insult to the national identity, it is Britain who did it; Britain knocked the Irish head and Britain used to word 'shift' to refer to the Irish women's underwear item. Therefore, now the Irish will have to go out of the Abbey Theatre and avenge their insulted identity. Moreover, the Irish now will become more romantic; for revolution is freedom and freedom is romanticism. If the audience is revolting against the facts, they are romantic. If they are revolting against romanticism, then they are too realistic and too religiously devoted. This is their picture, Shawn Keogh; too religiously devoted and too coward. And revolting against romanticism makes one realistic and more devoted to Christianity.

Synge put his audience in the "great gap between a gallous story and a dirty deed". If they rejected the gallous story, it becomes a dirty deed. Now the dirty deed will be romanticized and become a gallous deed. Synge intended his play to make the riots, so that the audience re-acted the play without noticing themselves doing it. Moreover, he intends to make a gallous story (his play) a dirty deed (to revolt against the British first of all by rioting, and then by knocking the father down). Then, this dirty deed is going to be a gallous deed by transforming it into a gallous story (through romanticizing history). This is how the national identity is built; revolution against the British, less religious devotion, transforming the real into romantic, and revolting against the ugly reality to make it a beautiful romance. Whatever, you Irish nationalists, find it deserves revolting for, go on and revolt against it. What is real is going to be romanticized, what is romantic is going to be real by revolting against it, now revolting against this new reality is romanticizing it again; the national identity is growing very rapidly in this way, and soon it will be recovered, and the

British will leave very soon. (One can think of the virtual revolutions on Facebook, and how they became real). To substantiate the argument that the riot is part of the main theme of the play, one has to quote Ben Levitas:'the Abbey became a room of mirrors; the audience part of the drama, ironically shouting down the action that they themselves perform'(qtd.in Schulze 78). This means that Synge intended his audience to revolt even against his own play, against him, and try to act the play themselves without noticing they are under Synge's control even while they are rioting.

The last message Synge wants the audience to know is " revolt". If you cannot revolt against the British now, revolt against me and my play. Then you will be able to revolt against the British; the riot inside the Abbey Theatre is a small revolution about everything bad in the Irish, and about the British occupation. Now being a mere incident, it will be like Christy's lie; it will grow very fast. At that time the Irish will be able to transform this small revolution into a big one as Christy transformed the lie into reality and was able to murder his father intentionally. At this time, revolution will not be in the Abbey Theatre, but will be a historical fact, which will be transformed into romanticism. All this completes the national identity.

One wonders of such a genius and also whether any another dramatist is able to bring his words into action before the audiences are out of the theatre. Synge indicates that the liberation of Ireland starts from the Abbey Theatre; he wants a cultural revolution to make the Irish ready for the real revolution, and then the real revolution comes back to the Abbey Theater to be romanticized.

Thinking of how quick Synge's mind is in moving from one idea to another, and I ask the dear reader what is the suitable word for this movement? "Shift"? Now you can say that your brain is similar to Synge's. For your brain is higher than thinking of the underwear item worn by a lady. He intended it to be understood in its triple meanings. It means cunning or intriguing a person, underwear item and movement to the other side. Therefore, Synge intended the audience to break up after the mentioning of the word "shift". Then, revolt when Christy used the word, which comes directly after murdering his father for the second time. This is the place in the play where the villagers are about to hang him. Synge used the word to give the spark for the riots; this means [and now we shift to our dear, nationalist audiences to see what they think]. They think as Synge himself. They should revolt. And that is what is going on stage. (Dear Professor, is it permissible to use an idea from Tom and Jerry here? When Tom was following Jerry, they enter the cinema to find the film is about them. Therefore, they relax and watch. Seeing himself overcome in the film, Tom follows Jerry to avenge his insulted identity.)

The purest race on earth is in Ireland. Even Christ himself came to our pagan Ireland and there he found himself as a whole man, where we romanticized his deeds and praised him and all for nothing till he discovered himself. Now even in Christian religion, the Irish are more Christian than Christ himself. Of course this meant to satirize the highly religious aspect of the Irish. Synge here refers to this play in particular, that what is true about the Irish in this play, is going to be romanticized; i.e., to be a hallmark of pride for the Irish as a national identity, what is not true is a romancing of the truth, which will turn to be a truth, and then romanticized and taken as national identity aspects. Synge found the Irish identity hovering in the space between realism and romanticism. When he wrote this play, he intended of giving the Irish national identity two wings—romantic and realistic—to go with them all over the world, travelling into the far places where the exotic is still to be found, and bringing it back to be claimed of as a national identity aspect. This does not mean that the national aspects he uses are not Irish, but it means to bring facts and to romanticize these facts. No matter how far Synge travels in land or space, what is important for him is to prove that the Irish are the noblest nation that has ever been on earth, and that they hate Christianity and love to be pagan once again. However, being now Christian, he urges the religious ones to be at least less religiously devoted than Christ himself. For he sees that religion is something related to the British, so the least of it would be the best.

> Christy. [His feelings hurt.] -- That's an unkindly thing to be saying to a poor orphaned traveler, has a prison behind him, and hanging before, and hell's gap gaping below.

Christy is an orphaned traveler; the most exotic and free kind of the Irish. He sees prison behind him, hanging in front of him and hell's gap gaping below. The fear of these things makes the Irish unable to free themselves. Far from mere speculations, number three is associated with the "three folded death" in Irish mythology; Christy anticipates prison, hanging and hell. This death is associated with the great warriors, gods, or even normal peasants. The significance of this unusual death, or torment in Christy's case, is to exaggerate the dangers in front of the hero, and to show the unrelieved enemy's malice even after the death of his opponent (Monaghan 400).

This can be understood in light of the modern reading of the play by Hyangsoon Yi, a Buddhist professor, who based her very brief analysis of the play on Victor Turner's Rites of Passage, who was influenced by Arnold Van Gennp. The last one studied many societies and observed how these societies develop. Victor Turner went in the same line, basing his studies on observation and on his predecessor's researches.

According to Turner, a developing personality in society goes in three main steps. Between the main steps, there are spaces which Turner stressed on. The main steps are transition, separation and re-aggregation (reunion). Liminality (from the Latin word limen which means threshold), is related to the middle stage of the above mentioned steps; separation. In this step, the initiand is stripped of everything related to his old identity: name, gender, class, property, clothes and social roles (Boltwood 2). Christy labels himself as an orphaned traveler. This means stripping him of his name and property. Moreover, the villagers try to define Christy on terms of his deed. Pegeen describes him as " a soft lad" which is a kind of stripping him of his masculinity. Yi argues that the initiand/person under development is subjected to "humiliation" and "ritual ordeals". This can be seen in Christy's character as being wandering for eleven days, facing the dangers of the road " facing hog, dog, or divil on the highway of the road.", hungry, tired and afraid. Moreover, when he describes his father's treatment of him, one can see more types of humiliation. In the final phase of this stage, the traveler, to call him, is characterized as full of paradoxes and in a middle stage between life and death (Boltwood 2). When the subject finishes this stage, he acquires a new identity; more stable personality and a higher social level he has not achieved before. This can be seen in Christy gaining attention gradually as the play goes on. The last stage is called "reaggregation", where the subject has found himself (Boltwood 2). Liminality is "defined as a realm of pure possibility whence novel configurations of ideas and relations may arise'." (2) Christ(y), who is supposedly, the most hated person to Pegeen (Pagan Ireland), and the traveller/tinker, whom Pegeen declares her fear of him and all his likes, now is being welcomed into her house. Christ(y) is emasculated to the utmost level by depicting two women competing to gain him and he is busy with his bread and milk and the stage direction tells the reader how he answers Widow Quin's greeting;[shyly]. Now the ground is ready for"Communitas…refers the 'homogeneity and comradeship' developed spontaneously among initiands who undergo ritual trials together in liminal seclusion."(2) Christy is feminine more than masculine, while Pegeen is more masculine than feminine. Christy acquires his not-yet-discovered masculinity by his contact with Pegeen, the masculine lady; if the term is strange, maybe feminist could suit her. Therefore, here is a place of high irony; the British, or even Christ(y) discovered their masculinity in Ireland. This leads to the fact that Britain was referred to as masculine and Ireland as feminine (Schulze 6). Synge is satirizing this masculinity as it had been given to them by an Irish lady. When one goes to see Christy's speech, though it has poetic style, is realistic, whereas Pegeen's speech is poetic and romantic. Moreover, to tell somebody of the bitter truth does not make a psychological change in him to discover his lost identity. One needs to glorify his small deeds, his (hated) name, and even his "small feet".

After all, Christy wonders "Is it me?" Then, he curses the mirror he has left at home; it did not tell him the truth of his handsome face. Shelley says exactly "poetry is a mirror which makes beautiful that which is distorted" (Ronsley 73). Therefore, Christy was "distorted" and Pegeen's mirror (poetry) made him see himself beautiful.

Christy's mentioning of a "mirror" and a "devil" is related to the fact that Christianity demonized the pagan gods, making them devils (Monaghan 142).

Christy being a devil at home, is a god-like figure in Pegeen's mirror: pagan gods are devils in Christianity, and devils in Christianity. Therefore, devils are gods in Pagan belief. Pegeen told him what made him see his face through Pegeen's eyes. She expressed what she saw in him into language, or a romantic language/poetry talk/oral speech to make him discover that he is handsome. Old Mahon describes his son as "an ugly young streeler". This means Christy is ugly but Pegeen's romanticism and poetry talk, made the ugly beautiful. When Shawn K tries to bribe Christy, he gives him new clothes. Widow Quin praises him, and the stage direction tells the reader that Christy is "as proud as a peacock". Next is Christy's clothing as a playboy. Finally, his celebration as a playboy. One would think that the opposite should happen; he should prove to be a playboy, and then be clothed as a playboy. It is always the romantic preceding the real. In other words, the community romanticizes an aspect, and Christy goes to aspire to suit him in the end. More precisely, romanticism is being made realism. When romanticizing stops, or even worse, the ugliest face of reality is shown to Christy—his father is alive, the community accuses him of being a lair and he is rejected by Pegeen—he is ready now to act his story and make it real.

Christ(y) is rejected by everybody in Ireland, then, he is ready to kill his father to marry his father's metaphorical wife; Pegeen: Old Mahon is Pegeen's husband. Since Pegeen is Cessair (Noah's kinswoman), and Old Mahon is

Pagan, who did not die in the Flood, as Jimmy assumes that they would say when the body had been discovered. Christy is an Oedipus in his all features. Moreover, if Christopher Mahon delivers itself to Christ of Her Man, Old Mahon delivers itself to Old Man. Seeing Christy at the end of the play reversing the social order and enslaving him, this can be interpreted as "by fostering communitarian values, liminality overhauls the dominant social order and provides the 'seedbeds of cultural creativity'."(Boltwood 3) the son going out enslaving the father is not accepted socially. Therefore, it is a loud cry in the faces of the Irish to run immediately out of the theatre to rearrange things. A boy who is nothing, but discovered himself by the help of Pagan Ireland, is now enslaving the Irish. Here Synge is examining the "dominant social order," (the Irish being occupied) "and provid[ing] the seedbeds of cultural creativity." (Revolution in culture or in reality for each one leads to the other).

Thinking of Pegeen, she starts the play, and when Christy enters, she romanticizes the story and the storyteller. When the story is discovered to be a lie, she reacts against it. This reaction against the lie is a reaction of a pagan lady against Christianity, which she sees as a lie. The lie is proved to be true, so she torments the murderer, as a kind of too much hatred for Christianity even though it is true; she does not need it. Now she is in the gap that separates reality and romanticism. When Christy goes out, Pegeen is more Pagan. She refuses to be engaged with somebody whom she was arranging for her wedding with in the opening lines of the play. She is now in complete divorce with Shawn Keogh for his devotion to Christianity and realism. After all, she is lamenting the playboy since he is the last romantic person in Ireland, who is not too religiously devoted to Christianity. Therefore, her lamentation over the playboy's loss is a cry against too much Christianity in Ireland, and too much realism, leaving her without any pagan romantic man. That is why she cries " I have lost the only playboy of the western world" (emphasis added). All his followers are more religious than him. Now Pegeen is lamenting for Christ(y) to save her from too much Christianity in her homeland. The word "only" in Pegeen's words refer to Christy as being Christ. For it is unbelievable to think of only one hero in the whole western world. This means also that the main theme is too much Christianity in Synge's homeland. Synge is still right about this lamentation; the Irish are more religiously devoted than all the European nations. At the same time, they are more nationalist/ patriotic than all the European nations. If Synge could not change much about the extremely religious aspect of the Irish, he made them aware of their national identity. However, what Synge satirized, he inadvertently recorded as a national aspect; the Irish extreme religious devotion.

Here are some quotations to substantiate the upcoming analysis of the play:

Turner's paradigm provides a particularly useful tool for explaining a recurrent pattern of interaction between the Traveler and the sedentary characters in Irish drama....Their encounter proceeds in three realms, be it nomadism or sedentarism; they momentarily lapse into liminal condition of an otherworldly borderland where their customary insider-outsider differences are abrogated; and they finally return to their respective former worlds. This movement approximates the ritual act of crossing the limen.... (Boltwood 4 emphasis added and the word means the stage of conscious feeling).

"...the motif of a spiritual journey tends to serve as a vehicle for dramatizing the psychological transformation triggered by the Traveler's visit" (Boltwood 3).

"In his most celebrated work of Synge's, the stranger from the road performs the dual role of acting as an agent of change for the peasants and also of becoming the object on which the settled can wield their metamorphic influence"(Boltwood 6).

"The following rejoinder of an Irish Darwinist from an Irish Presbyterian minister might almost pass for a derogatory reading of Christy's actions and motivations:

['The human subject constructed by 'the evolution hypothesis'] is not bound to do or refrain from doing because of any penalty attaching to conduct; if there be penalty affecting the individual at all, he may judge, perhaps, that in his present environment it is as often against the right action as in favor of it: he is not bound to subordinate the lower feelings to the higher; if the lower—being for most part more intense—yield him a greater sum of pleasure in this life, it is his duty […]to indulge in them: he is not bound to be truthful or honest; for though society is much injured by roguery and deceit, the harm wrought by his conduct would affect him little in comparison with the many advantages to be secured by his dishonesty gotten wealth" (qtd. In Burke 123).

This goes with Freud's psychoanalysis theory, when he says that "the id is primitive and needy…the ego develops out of the id…The super ego is representative of external, social influences upon the drives…" (Green 146).

In the light of the above quotations, one can go back to the play to find that Christy murdered his father (the id) and came to get married to his metaphorical mother. During the play, his ego is acquired, and now his super ego is leading his id. In other words, Christy murdered the national identity represented by his heathen/pagan father/the id and goes to marry the mother. At the end of the play, he goes out and the father/pagan/ Irish/ id, is enslaved by him. Christianity has controlled the primitivism of the Irish people. Therefore, the whole play, one might say, is about repressing the desires, the ego and super ego; about the Irishman's brain and how it is controlled by Christianity. " Communities in Synge's dramas eventually aspire to reinvigorate the spirit of folk culture as an antidote to the emotional importance and moral tyranny of petty middle-class norms and religious authoritarianism" (Boltwood 5) (emphasis added).

> Christy:"…going in strange places with a dog nosing before you and a dog nosing behind…""…groaning wicked like a maddening dog"

This imagery of dogs noising Christy is related to Cuchulain, whose name was acquired from the dog of Culan.

> Pegeen. You never hanged him, the way Jimmy Farrell hanged his dog…

> Christy…and I walking forward facing hog, dog, or divil on the highway of the road.

Now this imagery is to link the slain father with the imagery of a throttled dog; as Cuchulain did.

> Philly. The peelers is fearing him, and if you'd that lad in the house there isn't one of them would come smelling around if the dogs itself were lapping poteen from the dungpit of the yard.

The relatedness of dogs fearing Christy is again related to Cuchulain. Christy's residence with Pegeen is related to guarding her, which also has its counterpart in Cuchulain's myth; when he kills Culan's dog, he performs the role of a dog; guarding the man and his property as a compensation for slaying the dog, which the job was assigned to.

> Michael. You would, surely. If they're not fearing you, itself, the peelers in this place is decent droughty poor fellows, wouldn't touch a cur dog…

The literal meaning of the above quotation may be rephrased as "if you, Christy, were a "cur dog", the peeler would not hurt you". This again a kind of tying Christy with the dog, or even alluding to the myth of tying Cuchulain's name with the dog he slayed.

> Christy. …when I'd my full share I'd come walking down where you'd see the ducks and geese stretched sleeping…

Christy speaks of himself as a poacher/ hunter, this related to Cuchulain, especially geese, where in the myth, Cuchulain returns after hunting some geese.

The sports competition is related to Cuchulain, when he proves to be the best in all fields of sports. Christy's experience with Pegeen is similar to Cuchulain's, when the latter goes to learn more fighting skills from a woman, and returns.

Christy as if having two mothers is also related to Cuchulain; who is thought to be born by one and brought up by another.

Language of the play

"... the immediate perfective which is expressed in Irish English by using the temporal adverb "after" followed by a continuous form of the verb as in "He's after breaking the glass" 'He has just broken the glass'.... This structure ... on a source construction in Irish which uses the adverb tar éis 'after' with a non-finite verb form for the same purpose..." (Hickey 8).

Father Reilly's [after] read[ing] it in gallous Latin...

I'm [after] feel[ing] the last gasps quitting his heart.

Aren't we [after] mak[ing] a good bargain...

(Synge, 20)

The returns given above show typical instances of the immediate perfective construction of Irish English (Hickey 1995).

Do, does, don't, doesn't whole word

Is it often the polis [do] [be] coming into this place, master of the house?

The clumsy young fellows [do] [be] ploughing all times

The like of them [do] [be] walking abroad with the peelers

...the way the needy fallen spirits [do] [be] looking on the Lord?

"Synge took the language of rural Ireland and edited it in order to highlight certain qualities (strikingly concrete imagery, rhetorical delight in metaphor, alliteration, assonance, and rhythm) that he identified as deriving from Gaelic...[which are] characteristically oral"(Kearney 124).

" It was part of Synge's greatness that he realized... that the future of poetic drama did not lie within the limits of the traditional blank-verse form—that a new poetic medium needed to be forged, one which would combine the vigor and intensity of poetry with the flexibility and naturalism of prose. He found the ma-kings of such a medium in the Anglo-Irish dialect, and exploited them to the full" (Qtd. In Kearney 124).

Michael. Would you think

    Well to stop here and be

Pot-boy, mister honey,

    If we gave you good wages,

And didn't destroy

You with the weight of work?

Pegeen. [Very kindly and persuasively.] –

> Let you stop a short while anyhow. Aren't you destroyed walk[ing] with your feet in bleed[ing] blisters, and your whole skin need[ing] wash[ing] like a Wicklow sheep.

Michael. And begging your pardon, mister, what name will we call you, for we'd like to know?

Pegeen. Wasn't I telling you, and you

> A fine, handsome young fellow
>
> With a noble brow?

Christy. I did, God help me, and there

> I'd be as happy as the sunshine of St. Martin's Day,
>
> Watching the light passing the north or the patches of fog, till I'd hear
>
> A rabbit starting to screech and I'd go running in the furze.
>
> Then when I'd my full share
>
> I'd come walking down where

> You'd see the ducks and geese
>
> Stretched sleeping on the highway of the road, and before
>
> I'd pass the dunghill, I'd hear
>
> Himself snoring out, a loud lonesome snore
>
> He'd be making all times,
>
> The while he was sleeping, and he a man'd be raging all times,
>
> The while he was waking, like a gaudy officer you'd hear
>
> Cursing and damning and swearing oaths.

Finally, Synge's play is a mixture of ideas taken from the Old Testament, Greek Literature, Irish myths, the Bible and real life. It is left, then to mention that the main incident of the play has a real-life ground. When Synge was on the Aran Islands, he was told of a man who killed his father. There are three incidents which go in the same direction. There is no need to mention the details of them since all stress the fact the play has some historical facts. Having a historical background does not mean that Synge did not include other ideas in the play. Moreover, being a story similar to that of Oedipus, Synge was able to use the theme more freely. The story being related to psychoanalysis, Synge used Freud's ideas about supressing the primitive needs of the id in the human being by the ego. The language of the play is poetic but in the style of prose and the words are mostly translated from Irish into English, as Nicholas Grene is convinced, while other words are left without translation as "shebeen", "houseen", "poteen" and "banbhs". Synge's language—as he himself mentioned in the preface—as being taken from the mouths of the villagers, does not mean that the syntax is also taken from the villagers. However, he mostly used Anglo-Irish syntax with exceptions in order to give a poetic style, and to make the speech comprehensible for the audience. The most powerful themes in the play are, Christianity and its suppression of the id(entity) of the Irish, revolution, noble pagan race, satire of Christianity and Christian people, especially the devout, and a way of making a new national identity out of romancing reality then romancing the new reality to make it go into the nation's memory of historical heritage which makes the national identity.

If Christy is a Christ, Cuchulain and Oedipus, he is also a traveler. A traveler and a Cuchulain is to preserve national identity. Oedipus and Christ is to eliminate national identity. At the end, Oedipus is reconciled with his father. This leaves Christy as a Cuchulain and a Christ and both are associated with travels. However, Christ is realistic and Cuchulain is romantic. In this way, Synge managed to keep his theme of realism and joy to the very end of the play. Therefore, Christy's intentions of going romancing can be read as going fighting and making tales being told about his heroism. In this way, one can see how Synge tried to keep the balance between realism and romanticism to the end of the play. By doing so, he expressed the real situation in Ireland; Britain is realistic and Ireland is romantic. In the end of the play, Synge showed how romanticism leads realism by depicting the playboy leading his father. The Playboy, therefore, is a free person. That is why Pegeen laments losing him. He is a free Irish hero, so Pegeen/ Ireland needs him. Therefore, the play is a practical method of how the Irish free themselves. First of all, they have to raise the loy in front of their enemy. Of course the loy has historical connotations to the 1798 revolution. Many peasants joined the supporting French soldiers holding loys. Therefore, the general meaning becomes the raising of weapons in the enemy's face. The whole picture for Synge is a kind of skirmishes here and there and a matter of armed gangs shooting and escaping. Then, these groups will be applauded by the nation. This can be seen when Pegeen started the play in lamenting the loss of the people who opposed the law even with the smallest deeds. When Christy comes into the pub, the villagers try to discern his deed by a "guess the word" way. They suggest many possibilities, most of which are related to opposing the law and alluding to the colonial status of Ireland. Killing the father is always associated with the two opposing forces in the child's psyche; he wants to step away the father and take his place (a first urge) and the fear form castration. Christy overcomes his fear and gets rid of his fear. Moreover, the whole problem being about Widow Casey who is Christy's foster-mother, supports this argument.

Christy, in refusing to marry his mother and be an Oedipus, kills his father and becomes an Oedipus. This means to kill the father in the sake of the mother not in order to kill the father in order to marry the mother. In other words, to keep her chastity, to defend her by killing the oppressor. Purgatory has the same theme. For the mother's freedom, Christy killed his father. The way this happened was in front of the audience. Christy was initiated firstly by praising him until he loses his feminine qualities by the help of masculine women. Women represent romanticism and men represent realism. Christy was coward, but romanticizing his half masculine side made his masculine features show up. This can show how Synge kept the theme of realism and joy even in the characters' psyches. Romanticizing the masculine features means romanticizing realism. By romanticizing realism, we multiply this realism into being able to fill the gap that separates the romantic picture from the realistic one. An example is necessary in order to clarify the theme for in fear it is not so. If a coward man had a small dispute with another one, though he showed very little amount of courage, we praised it too much, the next time he will show more courage and so on until he fills the gap between our romantic praising, and his real actions. Our words become very real about his valor at the end. This is the way of making a hero. This theme, in addition to the theme of being mature under the women influence, are taken from Cuchulain's legend. When Cuchulain slayed the dog, courageous men went out and praised Cuchulains' valor. When he needed a further training, he went to a woman. When time of action comes, these trained men in Synge's school will be able to show their courage. And they did immediately before the play had ended. However, they need now just little praise and everything will be fine. The riots in the Abbey Theatre will be out, and the loy will be raised in the British soldiers' faces. Pegeen's lament now can be read as a cry from Ireland for such men to be trained and ready to fill the gap between word and deed. The Irish were known for their bragging about nothing. Synge wants them to be real pictures of their self-drawn images. Moreover, he celebrates everything even this bad side in the Irish is celebrated. He means to say that grand stories make grand warriors, grand talk makes heroes. Therefore, he brought his stories to the Abbey Theatre to build an Irish army. Even more, stories, when told, the Irish believed in bringing back the dead warrior's soul into life once again, and gave the storyteller the freedom of adding more details to the original story, but to keep its essence. This happens on stage; while the story is being told, it grows bigger, the hero grows with his story to the moment of which the hero is able to fill the gap between the story and the deed. At this moment, Pegeen tells him of the gap. In fact, Christy has now surpassed his story to the level of finishing levelling the gap before Pegeen discovers it. When Christy leaves, he is worthy of his story; a real deed and not just a mere story.

The Well of the Saints

The Well of the Saints gives the impression of Christian belief to the title. However, the title is of Synge's play, who is well-known of his subversion of the Christian belief when mentioning a religious theme. Therefore, the title means a place where water is holy. The rejection of the healing in the second time is a rejection of the holiness of this well and the will of the saint. Therefore, one can see how Synge meant the title to be understood; the well of the saints interferes in the Irish landscape and the saints oppose the will of God, thinking they are doing well. Moreover, the well might be holy before Christianity and was attributed to it later, as the shamrock; the symbol of Irish identity was attributed to St Patrick. This leads to the theme of Christening landscape and people in Ireland. Being holy and able to heal for a while, means that the well had this quality, but when saints interfered, it lost most of its healing power. When Martin refuses to be cured a second time, he refuses to see by Christian eyes and prefers blindness to seeing. If one moves to the setting, "in Ireland a century or more ago" leaves little doubt that it dates back to a period about 1800. However, it might be the Famine included in the play. Now the general line of argument.

By presenting most of the characters as travelers or tinkers, Synge represented one of the themes related to the general movement of the Traveler Drama in addition to the belief that tinkers represented the essence of the Celtic race. The saint, being also a traveler, has an historical implication. Many islands in Ireland were assigned to one saint, who had to travel regularly between them. Having two beggars is something related to tinkers in Ireland. Tinkers used to beg with their wives. Timmy, being a smith, means that he is also a tinker; most tinkers were smiths who were excelled in their metalwork. Tins and cans are mentioned too much for the historical fact that tinkers sold these objects. Martin mentions throwing a man in the bog after killing him and taking his money: "... and threw down his corpse into the bog ..." Archaeologists have recently discovered many corpses in bogs and discerned they were criminals or might be human sacrifices. Bogs were seen as places of the otherworld creatures. Many references were made to the shortage of food and starving animals. This leads to more confirmation that the play has some traces to the Famine period. Another historical fact is the fasting saint, who is described as a skin thrown on bones. The holy water has historical implication. Many wells in Ireland are looked at as holy, and people go there for sacrificing something, giving coins or drinking water. The beggars being on the cross roads is an historical fact. Many beggars during the Famine particularly, gathered at the roadside. Martin's flirting with Mary goes to the heart of Celtic custom and is mentioned by Synge heavily; in Celtic custom, it was thought that leaving the host's wife with the guest is a kind of hospitality;" Sharing one's slaves-and perhaps one's wife-with visitors was probably part of what a hospitable host offered to make guests feel welcome." (Clancy 60). Moreover, the theme of penalty can be found in Celtic myth. When one is healed, he has to pay for being cured (236). This theme is found in the play when the blind couple find trouble after being healed, and return blind again. Refusing to be healed is a kind of fear of paying the penalty which goes to the heart of Celtic culture in general, and Shamanism in particular. When looking into the dramatist's view point concerning the meaning of the blind couple, it can be seen as a kind of rejecting Christian belief and the way one looks at the landscape, the human life, and way of life. Seeing the couple healed for the first time and for a while, this reminds one of the <u>Playboy of the Western World</u>. When Christy murders his father, it was a story. However, the second time was real. The first time was romantic, the second was realistic. This time, the first time is realistic, the second time represents rejection of realism. When facing realism, the couple was shocked. This made them retreat into romanticism. For the surface looker, the rejection of being cured seems acceptance of realism. By making one's realism romantic, is romanticism. When looking into the general line of argument, it looks as if Synge wanted to say that blindness and Irishness is better than seeing and Christianity. To put it another way, to be Irish in thought is better than being a Christian believer. Moreover, what can be seen in the general line of argument is that national identity is preserved in what is known as the natural resources of Ireland. When Martin flirts Mary Byrne, he wants to bring her into the woods and mountains. He wants to take her into the countryside and make her one of the tinkers who travel on the roads; tinkers. The saint, being a traveler, means that he has some resemblances to St Patrick whom the tinkers claim to be taking his way of life. While the tinkers are usually known for their travel, these beggars start their travel at the end of the play. They are forced by the community to leave. This gives hints to the uprooted people in Ireland, who were driven out of their lands by the Penal Laws. This is also related to the post-Famine period. "Ditch" is a commonly used word in Synge's plays. It is used thirty times in four plays. It means, for the Irish, a " (reminiscent of a shallow grave)". "Not everyone enjoyed individual burial: some corpses, particularly those of children, were simply placed in ditches." (Lees 2). It is also related to the 1798 revolution; all those found on roadways or ditches were killed (Reamonn 3). It might have some religious meaning such horse temple (Monaghan 313). In this way, one can leave the historical to the mythical.

In Celtic myth, having a special talent, means to pay the penalty some way or another. Martin, being able to see in his mind, lost his sight. While those who have their sights lost their mind eyes. This can be clarified when looking to the way he objects to their lives when he saw them. He saw the realistic picture gloomy. But when he was looking to the same picture with his mind's eye, he saw it romantic. This means that the ugly can be turned beautiful by looking into it by the mind's eye. Normal eye gives the picture of real things in life to the mind, but when the mission is given to the mind to find the suitable picture depending on words, it gives a romantic view. When looking into things by the mind's eye, one can see the romantic, but real eye sees the real. Christian eye sees the romantic realistic, but the Irish eye sees the realistic romantic. Seeing for a while and then being blind again, helped the couple to be less romantic and more realistic in order to make a balance between romanticism and realism. This Synge's best discovery. When the couple wish to see, their wish is fulfilled, and then wish to be blind, which is bestowed too. This means romanticism leads realism. When realism and romanticism struggle over the couple, romanticism overcomes realism. When Christian realism tries to kill the Irish romanticism, Irish romanticism is saved by rejecting Christianity.

Looking into the play from the Celtic-Buddhist view, one can say that the play starts with the couple being happy for a degree. When they hear of being healed, they start to quarrel. Later on, they make a dispute for craving of being lovely and young again, and of having beautiful match. These events, in addition to the suffering at work, make the crisis of their suffering due to their craving. When they stop to crave, the suffering stops. This moment is achieved when they refuse to be healed. At this moment, they start their romantic journey.

Looking into the play from the view point of the traveler drama, one can find that the outsider this time is a saint. This means that the expected change is in religious belief. Therefore, healing the couple is a kind of baptism. However, when the couple reject the saint's prescription, they reject his authority over them. This rejection is a kind of self-freedom. This time, the rejected authority is a representative of the church. This gives a direct allusion to Britain. However, the rejection is rejecting being cured in eyes in order to preserve the mind's eye. Normal eye is being healed by a saint in order to see the world from a Christian point of view. While the mind's eye sees the picture from the Irish point of view. In other words, they refuse to see the world by Christian eyes. This means they want to keep what is left of Irish identity untouched by Christian belief. As for the matter of national identity in its broadest meaning, it is conveyed in the play by the couple. They married due to love and not like Timmy the smith and Molly Byrne. They are tinkers and beggars; the essence of Irish identity and preserver of an historical fact. They speak romantic language and refuse Christian thought and view of life. Due to the fact that the outsider is a saint, the main theme of national identity this time is religion. Christian religion is looked at as something threatening the Irish imagination of their lives. It makes their world too realistic, so they need a romantic mind. The problem, then, is in the Irish mind. This opens the discussion of psychoanalysis.

The first stage can be interpreted as an id stage due to the fact that the couple are romantic and in need of being healed, in addition to being imaginative. The second stage is the ego; when the child starts to form an image of the world around him. The last phase is a return to the id; where the self-image is uncorrupted by the senses. McGrath explains this by indicating that "the power of language to un-say the world, to speak it otherwise is crucial in a colonial situation. Whether defined as a social imaginary, an imagined community, or a performative enunciation, it is the only route to liberation" (41). Again, Hugh is quoted in the same reference declares that '...we must never cease renewing those images ["facts of history"]; because once we do, we fossilize'(45). Therefore, the couple only opened their eyes to refresh those facts of history and return blind again. The Irish mind is closed upon treasures of national identity. It has to be opened every now and then in order to be refreshed, and reclosed again. This refreshing happens by seeing some realistic things, and closing eyes again. This way, the Irish mind can remake the realistic romantic. They saw Christianity, so they have to romanticize this realistic belief by closing their eyes after seeing some realistic things.

When looking into the details, there is a blind couple, a saint and other characters. The blind couple being the center of the play, means the main theme is the blindness of the couple. Blindness is a symbolic paganism. When refusing to be cured, it means refusal to convert into Christianity. Blindness makes the brain dark, and being so, it preserves the things it got for a long time. They open their eyes to refresh their views of the world and close them again. By doing so, they have normalized the scale between realism and romanticism. In being wife and husband, means also realism and romanticism. The romantic and realistic are balanced. When the case is so, romanticism takes the lead. The couple leaves the community, but as in The Playboy, the couple is triumphant.

The language of the play is Anglo-Irish especially in syntax but not in vocabulary.

> Mary Doul. It isn't going to the fair, the time they **do be driving** their cattle and they with a litter of pigs maybe **squealing** in their carts, they'd give us a thing at all. (She sits down.) It's well you know that, but you must **be talking**.

In addition to the form of "do+be+verb+ing" and the continuous phrases linked by "and", language is also poetic.

> Timmy. If I'd a mind I'd be telling you of a real
>
> **W**onder this day, and the **way**
>
> You'll be having a great **j**oy,
>
> Maybe, you're not thinking on at **al**l.

More examples can be clarified, but this is enough and the rule can be taken to cover the whole play. Even in language, Synge uses the romantic and realistic wings. His language is poetic, mostly due to the Anglo-Irish style and the vocabulary is real. Vocabulary is used to express real peasant people. Such examples include mentioning of agricultural tools, animals, woods, and landscape in general.

The language of the play, then, is associated with the general theme in the play. Moreover, has some traces to Celtic-Buddhism in the theme of stopping to crave for seeing and being satisfied with one's condition. In this line, the couple was blind due to craving for being able to see. When they were granted this wish, suffering has to show on the surface. When they feel they are comfortable in being blind, their trouble comes to an end.

National identity in the play is associated with the theme of blindness. When the couple refuses to be cured, they refuse to be christened. In this way, they preserve their Irish identity by rejecting Christianity. The couple represents any Irish couple. Therefore, the play portrays a call upon the Irish to reject the Christian way of looking into Irish identity. What makes one regard the rejection of being cured is a rejection of being Christian or adopting the Christian view of the world is the fact that

> The healing spring near the center, once the place for celebration on Midsummer's Eve, now represented a place for renewal. The ancient bronze bell excavated there was copied to hang by the well-waters of patron St. John the Baptist, whose feast is June 24th; venerable symbols of Christian monastic bell and Tibetan dorjé striker unify two holy practices.

The above quotation is taken from an article emphasizing the existence of what is now being called Celtic-Buddhism. Therefore, the well is related to Celtic-Buddhism and the bell, which in its turn, has the same reference due to associating it with the well and the saints at the same time. This gives one a picture of a Celtic-Buddhist well and bell, being taken by Christianity. Another substantive quotation; "holy bells of Ireland are of distinct Buddhist shape, being of an irregular cylindrical form, as in India, etc., and not round as in Christian lands "(Murphy 152). Therefore, the saint is Christian in his religious belief, but he uses Celtic-Buddhist tools; the bell and the holy water. Monaghan also mentions the fact that holy wells were so before Christianity (471). Some Celtic divinities slipped into the books with their names preceded by the label "saint" (405). In Celtic myth, wells, and especially holy ones, were thought to have the ability of treating the sick and they are revered to this day, with about 3000 holy wells in Ireland. Most of them were attributed to saints though they were sacred before Christianity. Trying the cloak with the bell on Martin before the saint comes is another indication of Christianity's attempt to Christianize all the Irish aspects. Here, one can have little doubt that the real intended meaning is national identity.

When looking at the play from the angle of national identity, one can see that the play has many themes related to cultural nationalism. Martin's misconception of his wife is an example of the Irish man being unable to know his identity and the identity of his wife. When he was looking at his wife by his mind's eye, she was beautiful, and he thought of himself as handsome too. When he describes the girls, he knows their beauty before seeing them by his eyes. However, when he is healed and given the opportunity by a saint to be cured in order to look at himself and the others, the picture is demonized. This is what Synge meant to say. Christianity demonized and debased the sacred and beautiful in the eyes of the Irish. Christianity normalized the romantic, so it became ugly.

In this line, one can add that the general argument of the play is about the power in the water from the well. This power means the power of the national identity since it comes from the deep ground up to the surface. As for being rising after burying the saints, it means the shallowness of Christianity in comparison of national identity. Moreover, the saints might be of Celtic-Buddhist origin as it is the case with many legendary people being claimed belonging to the church. The power of curing attributed to the holy wells in Ireland was thought to have a stronger power in certain days. When the play opens, Martin and his wife were waiting for those coming from the fair to give them some money. The saint, being a traveler and on the island during the fair, refers to the myth of the dead or otherworld fairies coming to this world in order to take somebody who is still alive. Bringing the water from a place where former living people are now buried, means the reverence of the dead, and the adoption of the former generations' look onto life. Martin and his wife's blindness for a second time is a metaphorical symbolism of the shortsightedness of Christianity in comparison with Irish nationalism. Moreover, the small effect of this water is an allusion to the small effect Christianity has done upon national identity.

> Molly Byrne. It'd be a fine thing if someone in this place could pray the like of him, for I'm thinking the water from our own blessed well would do rightly if a man knew the way to be saying prayers, and then there'd be no call to be bringing water from that wild place, where, I'm told, there are no decent houses, or fine-looking people at all.

This finishes the dispute over whether the well is sacred due to the saints or it is so before Christianity. Molly is indicating very clearly the sameness of water whether it was taken from the nearby well or the far one, where she was told there were no decent people. Then, the saints are not decent people or fine looking ones. However, she attributes most of the water's power to the ability of good prayer. The prayer is Spanish which can be translated to be approximately "Oh, saint who is sitting in the underworld, come, you spirit, now, and grant the miserable health". In fact, the prayer is a ridicule of Christianity as it is always the case with Synge; whenever religion is mentioned, he subverts the theme against the church. To return to the prayer, it indicates, by the mouth of the saint, that his fellows are now in Hell. Moreover, he conjures these spirits to heal Martin. Now if one returns to Molly's suggestion of using water from the nearby well, but one has to know how to say a prayer, one can figure what Synge meant. A curse on the saints will do the job. For more accurate translation, here is the sentence if one is excelled in Spanish he can figure out more than me.

> Saint. [Solemnly.] Laus Patri sit et Filio cum Spiritu Paraclito Qui Suae dono gratiae misertus est Hiberniae. . .

Therefore, the saint's words are taken from Celtic myth. Celts believed that water places were the border lines that separate this world from the world of the dead. These borderlines can be crossed by the dead and the living—mostly by mistake for the latter—at certain festivals. Here is one of the momentous occasions in the play. Christianity is prospering over the Celtic heritage, and Christening the national identity. This is an historical fact. For the Celtic myths were written by Christian hands, and being so, most of the legends and tales were modelled to go with the general moral teachings of Christianity. Not only tales, but wells, shamrock and other plants, hills, temples, Irish cross, gods became devils and others became saints. What Christianity did is that it altered Irish national identity and claimed it as Christian. What can be read from the little effect of the water is that Christian effect on national identity and the

Christian view to life are short-lived. Moreover, Christian influence is little over national identity, and soon will disappear. The rejection of being cured a second and permanent time is a rejection of the Christian identity to substitute Irish identity. The villagers expel the couple to live a tinker's life; they have returned to the very essence of national identity representative. Tinkers, travelers, romantic and rebels against Christian faith and identity.

In this regard, one can see how the play provides a way of preserving the Irish national identity by taking the blind couple as an exemplar. They begin their journey as tinkers in order to celebrate the beauty of landscape, and to emulate the first Irish traveler. They also reject Christianity and its look on the universe and social life. In general, a tinker's life is romantic, and a sedentary life is realistic. In substituting the sedentary with nomadic, they free themselves from the influence of any kind applied upon them by the colonizers. The tinkers until this very day are still enclosed communities in Europe in general and make an ongoing problem for governments concerning the places where they build their caravans in cities, the way of teaching their children, the way of taking precautions for hygiene and so on. Therefore, they preserve their own way of life until this day because of their distance from the center of social life in the world.

Taking the play in general, one can see that it starts with the couple in need of seeing the world, then being disappointed with what they saw. Finally, they return blind again. Again, like The Playboy, romanticism, realism and finally romanticism again. The gap mentioned in the stage directions has a relationship with the gap between realism and romanticism. In the first Act,

> [Roadside with big stones, etc., on the right; low loose wall at back with gap near center; at left, ruined doorway of church with bushes beside it. Martin Doul and Mary Doul grope in on left and pass over to stones on right, where they sit.]
>
> Mary Doul. What place are we now, Martin Doul?
>
> Martin Doul. Passing the gap.

In the third Act,

[The same Scene as in first Act, but gap in center has been filled with briars, or branches of some sort...] this gap is a representative of the symbolic gap that separates realism and romanticism. In the first Act, there is a gap in the wall, but in the third Act, it is closed with bushes. The ridge between realism and romanticism is bridged, and romanticism has to take the lead. When realism and romanticism become the same, this means that national identity is in its best situation for Synge. He stressed in the preface of The Playboy that one "has to have realism and one has to have joy". Moreover, Synge's plays depend upon the difference of realism and romanticism. He builds the romantic, strengthens the real, until the real and the romantic has nothing to separate them. He gives the lead to romanticism and the curtain falls. In other words, he wants to bridge the gap between the mythic and historical until history and myth has nothing to separate them. After that, he gives the lead to the dramatist to lead the church. He wants to fasten history to Celtic myth, and associate the two with real life. Then, bring the church under his rule, to find at the end that the Abbey Theatre is leading Ireland, with a remote history and a mythical past, in addition to the church, all under his command. In this way, romanticism leads realism in past, present and future. Synge is convinced in Yeats' pint of view that the dramatist should lead the church and politics in general, but differs with Yeats in that he gives the lead to the tinker, who, in turn, gives it to the thinker. In this way, one can find how Synge is more accurate and faithful in building a national identity that Yeats. Synge wants the tinker teach him, and he presents to the Irish what he has learned from the tinker. Yeats wants the tinker to listen only to the thinker. In this line, one can find how Synge is more realistic in his drama, and how his stories and words are taken from the mouths of people he wrote about. Synge's primary master is not Yeats, but a tinker. While Yeats is a master of a tinker and a thinker. In this way, one can see how the dramatists in the Abbey Theatre acted their own plays without noticing. It is true, Yeats is Synge's master in regard of the theme of national identity. Therefore, Yeats is the thinker and Synge is the tinker. This can be substantiated by an historical fact which some critics deny while others confirm. It is concerned with whether Yeats who advised Synge to go to the Aran Islands. From this analysis, it seems that this is real. Therefore, the thinker advised the tinker (Synge). Synge learned from the real tinkers and returned to the thinker. In this way, Synge moved between realism and romanticism, and his real life is an application of his own discovery.

In this play, one has seen that the national identity in Ireland is being claimed to be Christian. What Christianity has done is only putting its touch on the national aspect and is turned to be Christian one. Synge in this another play, presented his view of how drama should be; a mixture of realism and romanticism. The conclusion is as usual, occurs when the gap which separates realism and romanticism is bridged. The time romanticism and realism are reconciled, the curtain falls. This is to indicate that the curtain is the only borderline between the world on the stage and the audiences. When romanticism and realism are reconciled and bridged, romanticism takes the lead. In other words, the play is what should affect the audience after the end of the play. This another theme, in addition to the previously mentioned one during The Playboy riot, where Synge tried to bridge the gap which separates the audience from the play. It reached with him to the degree of having them act his play before they went. This time, he was satisfied to leave the curtain, but with little influence after the fall of the curtain. Although he was a man of genius and made his audience shout upon a thing they themselves were performing inadvertently, he did not notice that his life is an application of his plays including Riders. In this play, what one does is related to his destiny. While in the other plays, the action is a mixture of romance and realism to the end when romanticism and realism are in the same level with nothing to separate them. This is also Synge's life which was a mixture of the two, until he found that his masters are the tinker and Yeats the thinker. Therefore, did Synge intend to make his life a mixture of the two? It must have been written for him. What Synge left behind is a small number of plays, but we are still learning from them even though their age is now more than a century. However, one has to find if Synge wrote the first plot or was it written and he acted it. Certainly he was the actor in his life with the plot depending on the same theme of his own plays. This brings one to the phrase which I have no documentation for, but heard it from my supervisor; life is drama and drama is life. Now whether for the dramatist his life is his own drama looks for me to be possible in Synge's case. His life and work had nothing to separate. Therefore, romanticism and realism; his plays and his life, are inseparable. When he spoke of romanticism taking the lead, he might be alluding to death as the opening gate where one goes into Heaven. Synge's life, then, is the same as his plays to the degree of being impossible to separate his life and his plays. This reminds one of Synge's most recurring phrase; "one has to have realism and one has to have joy". Synge's life (realism) and his plays (romanticism/ joy) cannot be separated. Therefore, Synge applied his theory in his life and work.

Juno and the Paycock

The play is about the 1921 Anglo-Irish Treaty and the Civil War in 1922, which was sparked by the Treaty. Being written carelessly, the Treaty's application formed the most challenging problem in front of the newly established Free State. The Irish were divided into two parties; one supporting and another objecting to it, and went to arms in order to settle the dispute. The Treaty's vague words made an ambiguity to the concerned parties of how to apply it, though it was proposed to substitute the confusing words with clear ones but in the same meaning. O'Casey commented on the Treaty and added that what was proposed by one of the negotiation sides added nothing and took nothing from it. This is best shown in the wording of the will in the play which took nothing and added nothing, but the will ended as worse than nothing. Mrs Madigan says the police that they are not better than what they had been during the British Government. This is related to the details of the Treaty; the military forces in the new regime are the same old organizations, but the leader changed. The same is for the complaints about the CID (Criminal Investigation Department) which its role was to quench any rebellious action against the British Government also continued its work in the Free State (Boltwood 50). The spies had the ugliest impression in the Irish minds. There are references to spies or double agents in the play; Nudget and Johnny. Mr Boyle refers to spies in his complaints about being followed wherever he goes. The influence of church on the Irish is mentioned as being allied to the strengthening of the British control on the Irish by using religious figures in political affairs. Religious figures' influence on politics and general life of the Irish continued in the Free State. Mentioning of Consoles by Boyle is related to the universal economic market the Irish are about to participate in. the gramophone is a technological device imported in order to refer to the invasion of the Irish market with the British goods. The assassinations and neighbors' shooting of each other are also historical facts. All these historical details are portrayed, but with little criticism. The situation is depicted but not in a satirical tone. Rather, to show real facts only as they are.

The most nationalistic aspects in the play are related to Catholicism, as a main religion of the Irish, the Irish language and culture. In other words, the Irish national identity in all its forms. In the following analysis, it will be dealt with religion and culture while the Irish language is to be delayed until discussing the language of the play in general. The audiences see a picture of the Virgin, the statue and the votive light when the curtain rises. Mary looks into the mirror and when she does not look into the mirror she looks in the paper. The stage directions mention something about her personality being under development by the influence of literature and under the suppression of the circumstances. When Mr. Boyle tells Joxer what Mary reads, one can know in what way Mary is developing; the self-realization of the woman and her freedom including sexual affairs. "… perhaps Ibsen's message concerning the oppression of women in society speaks most powerfully to her " (Boltwood 50). One could see that O'Casey intends to show the decline of national identity in this image. However, the opposite is right here; the return to national identity is meant through this idea, especially if one takes into consideration that Christianity and these books do reconcile. These books are not enough for Mary in order to develop into a full-realized personality; she needs the Traveler. Here one can put this play in the general line of traveler drama, and Bentham is the traveler. Being a theosophist, this means that the main transformation is to be expected is in religion. To substantiate the argument that Bentham's visit to the Boyles is meant to be a return into real national identity, one has to associate Bentham's religious beliefs into Celtic myth or Celtic culture in general.

Theosophy is the Buddhist's method of unifying himself with the universe. Bentham mentions Yogi; a person who comes into unity with the universe by fasting and purifying his soul. The main principles of this religion is the meditation in order to find the Life Spirit. However, this religion is accused of being a phallic worship. The relationship between Buddhist and Celtic beliefs can be seen in the "Round Towers, looming with sexual potency and exotic provenance, serv[ing] as a synecdoche for Ireland's supposed removal from taints of European rationality and imperial domination."(Murphy 7) Kilts argues that "the Buddha confirms the lineage of Celtic Buddhism as a lineage rooted and interlaced with the earth."(16). This is enough for establishing the relationship between Buddhism and Celticism. If one wishes for more details, they can refer to Celtic-Buddhism.org. Since Christianity is associated with emasculation and Buddhism with sexual worship, this means that the transformation of the characters' psyches is mainly related to the theme of sex.

When Bentham is asked about ghosts, he answers according to his theosophist belief; the whole thing is a required spiritual power in order to kill, a person with certain psychological features comes again to the place of crime and sees the whole affair. When Johnny enters his room, he sees Robbie Tancred kneeling in front of the statue. This is related to Celtic myth where it was believed that the dead returned to claim the living. Moreover, this is a Buddhist theme of about how ghosts are seen. This means that Johnny has started in his initiation in order to be transformed into a Buddhist. "A life in the spirit that combines with noble devotion and capacity for self-sacrifice shows rosy pink or light violet colors."(Steiner 165). That is why Johnny is highly concerned with the votive light. More astounding theme can be seen in "remembering means experiencing something that is no longer there, linking a past experience to my present life."(68) This means that Johnny assassinated Robbie Tancred while he was praying or kneeling in front of the statue of the Virgin. That is how different religions and their consequences are shown in the play.

The party in the Boyles family and the funeral in the Tancreds are the best circumstances for psychological development. Buddhism is associated with joy and for this reason the gramophone was played when the funeral passed. The funeral and the party associate with the world of fairies/ the otherworld and this world; funerals are related to the otherworld, and music and dancing are thought to be permanently going on in the fairy lands. The ghost which Johnny sees, is an idea related to myth; in certain festivals, the dead return to the world of the living to take somebody else. The same phenomenon is explained by Bentham that it is a matter of released power during the crime, which was stored in the air. When somebody passes the scene of the crime, he sees the whole thing. However, what is common to both is the fact that not everybody is able to see the ghosts unless he has unusual spiritual abilities. This leads to the conclusion that Johnny has such ability. He is a Buddhist; "some texts suggest that a kind of yoga was practiced by druids who, holding themselves in specific postures, spoke their prognostication."(Monaghan148). This means that Johnny is a Yogi; the highest member in Buddhism.

The withdrawal of religion is revealed by Mr Boyle when he compares the fame of Charlie Chaplin to the fame of priests. He then attacks the church's role in preventing the Irish from achieving their independence. Later on, when he is a man of money, he sees the church as an important organization, which had its role in the battle for freedom. Therefore, the relationship with the church depends on privileges not on faith in this religion. This means, in order to move into a higher social class, one has to have a good relationship with the church; the church has become the ministry of employment or more, the Father is the prime minister who is responsible for assigning all the effective roles on the Free State. Therefore, Christianity is the religion of politics and not the religion of the individuals. Since the country was divided upon sectarian division or difference, religion becomes the only means by which one can be a prominent figure. Christian principles shift in the same direction politics heeds. It is the Captain's alleged ship hit by winds from all the directions.

Mary looks into the mirror and the newspaper means a renewed Cathleen; the death of Tancred has transformed her. By her mirror, she can see the whole incidents in the state; the paper gives the news of what is going on, and the mirror to tell someone about their personality; physical features. Mrs Boyle is described in the stage direction of being beautiful before twenty years. This is another Cathleen Ni Houlihan. In the final lines of the play, Mary mentions her child being fatherless, to which Mrs Boyle replies "it will have better than a father, it will have two mothers" the child, is, again, a Cuchulain. The child being related to Christianity and Theosophy means that he will have a religion close to Christianity but will love his sexual potency and not reject or suppress it as it is the case with Christianity. To elaborate this theme is really associated to the Celtic myth, one has to mention that the symbol of sexual power in the Celtic culture is the male goat. St. Patrick was portrayed as a goatherd. Moreover, there is a statue in Ireland, which was thought to be one of the giants', holding two huge stick, but emasculated. It is thought that the absence of the giant's genital organ is related to opposition of Christianity (Monaghan 200).

To go back to this child, but equipped with the relationship between Buddhism and sexual power; Buddhism and sexual or phallic worship are related to each other. This boy is going to be Cuchulain, his mother is Mary; semi-Christ and will have sexual desire.

The idea of having a child out the institution of marriage came to the Celts when Christianity arrived. Moreover, Monaghan mentions that this is the case in all over the world except in certain communities, which are smaller in number to those who do not consider marriage as something necessary (123). By uniting Christianity to phallic worship, O'Casey returned to the previous religion in Ireland; Celtic-Buddhism. By this way, he associates Ireland with the whole world, culturally and spiritually. Culturally, by making references to authors from foreign countries, movie stars, and music, and spiritually, by associating the whole country with the whole universe in a unifying religion that precedes Christianity. This unifying religion is not only unifying of being older than Christian division in the country and being believed in India or the East in general, it is unifying through its teachings; the experienced Yogi is in complete unity with the universe by uniting his spirit to the Life Breath.

To the child again, the child's father is a Theosophist and his mother is hardly Christian or Catholic is particular. It is believed that the child is going to inherit his parents' spiritual as well as physical features. Moreover, the child spirit stores his parents' experiences and adds to these experiences his own. Then he passes the whole wisdom into the next generation and so on so forth. If one come to be acquainted with one of the mentioned works of Ibsen, they will see this theme clearly. Maybe in <u>Ghosts</u>; the father's sexual affairs, or the desire to have such, goes to the child. Even worse, the lady who was working in the house as a servant, was impregnated by the father and when the son comes back, he tries to have a sexual affair with her daughter. In this work, Ibsen tries to show that the desire for sex is similar to genetic inheritance. "In each life the human spirit appears as a repetition of itself, with the fruits of its experiences in earlier lifetimes. Thus this lifetime is the repetition of others, and brings with it what the spirit self has gained in its previous life." (Steiner 81) Therefore, the child is going to be a Cuchulain who will have his father's wisdom and sexual desire. In this way, he divorces Christianity forever. Religion is Celtic-Buddhism and adultery substitutes marriage or Christian celibacy. "Celtic Buddhism is an intermingling of the openheartedness of Buddhism and the open-endedness of the spiritual quest with the integration of living the mythic journey."(Murphy 19). Freedom for O'Casey means freedom of belief and freedom of individual thinking and behavior, and not only freedom from the British. It also means to open your arms to the world, not to be enclosed in your country and controlled by corrupt church members.

Language of the play is Dublin dialect. Here are some example, but not too much since the same was explained in earlier play. The more complicated analysis of the plays is to be later on in another paper, maybe, God willing.

Mr Boyle. But you shouldn't be frettin' the way you are; when a woman loses a man, she never knows what she's afther losin', to be sure, but, then, she never knows what she's afther gainin', either.

The first feature of Anglo-Irish syntax is the use of the formula be fretting; infinitive verb to be, a main verb ending with ing. Another feature is the use of "after" to substitute the present perfect tense as shown in this quotation. The pronunciation of "h" after the "t" and "d" letters. In the same line, Mr Boyle misunderstands an Irish sentence related to nationalism as being a prayer. Also Mr Boyle and Joxer confuse the Irish author A. M. Sullivan with the Irish-American boxer John L. Sullivan (Boltwood 56). This is related to the intended theme by O'Casey that the old historical heritage of the Irish State is eroding in front of the influence of new cultures including the erosion of the Irish language.

However, this is not too bad; one has to live in this big universe and communicate with it by culture and language. What O'Casey laments here is the openness of the Irish to new cultures and language while forgetting theirs. That is why Juno is in the play; to reconnect Mary to the history of Ireland, and Mary connects to the universe. In other words, Juno connects past to present, Mary is the medium by which past and future are connected. In this way, past, present and future are to be conveyed to the would-be-born child. What is astonishing is that Mary who corrects the real meaning of the Irish sentence to her father. This means she knows Irish, but through learning it at school not from her parents;

she will teach her child the Irish language. In this way, the child is a symbol of a completely restored national identity.

Mrs Madigan is a midwife; she witnessed Mary's birth. This means she is associated with prophecy. Moreover, she expects Mary to be an unusual person due to certain features noticed during her birth.". . .the new arrival of the Boyle's ud grow up a hardy chiselur if it lived, an' that she'd be somethin' one o' these days that nobody suspected, an' no signs in it…".

The child being without a father, with two mothers, means he is Cuchulain. Cuchulain was born from a relationship between a god and a queen. This means that his father is a god. Mary, being the daughter of Juno, is another indication in the same line; Juno is a Roman goddess and Mary being her daughter, goes in the same line. Christianity is the child of Buddhism. A relationship between a Buddhist and a Christian is a return into Buddhism; Christianity does not tolerate sexual power, whereas Buddhism worships it. The relationship is a complete rejection of Christian emasculation and control over sexual potency, and even the real application of this worship.

In succumbing to the sexual desire, Mary succumbs to the desires of the id. By this relationship, Mary expressed her full identity. This identity is expressed by the absence of the oppressive forces mentioned at the very beginning of the play represented by circumstances. Circumstances are the ego; since the ego is the outer self which one expresses to the others, while suppressing the desires of the id. Therefore, the ego was suppressed in Mary.

What forms the suppressive ego is the religious beliefs and social customs. Mary, in doing so, she reveals her full identity, her national identity. What was hindering Mary from revealing her identity freely is religion and customs. In doing so, Mary rejects religious influence on her and associates herself to the customs found everywhere in the world. Moreover, in doing this, she does not give away her national identity; on the contrary, she embraces it. Mary's religion is Celtic-Buddhism, which indicates the phallic worship. This means the utmost return to primitivism; the id is primitive and desiring. Therefore, Mary has returned to her true id(entity). Here one can refer to the fact that Mary is Ireland, and Juno is another Cathleen Ni Houlihan; this can be found, as stated earlier, in the stage directions which mentions Juno's beauty before twenty years from now.

The child makes the matter clearer. He is Cuchulain, the mythical hero of the Celts, he will be able to speak Irish; Mary knows it and this knowledge will be either inherited by the child or taught to him by his mother, his father is a Theosophist; the parents committed adultery, the experience will be passed to the child, and all the father's wisdom too. Above all, his father's religion is concerned with phallic worship. This is the complete national identity being restored. The language is Irish, religion is Celtic-Buddhism; church has no influence on individuals, and the born child is a hero. These are all the national identity features in one nationalist person. Just to make clear, this does not mean that O'Casey intends to indicate that sexual potency is the most important national aspect, but he is uneasy about Christianity's control over the individual to the level of controlling his sexual power. Moreover, in this way, he restores the national psyche to the id because the ego, represented by Christianity, has forbidden the id(entity) from expressing itself to the outer world. In this way, O'Casey made the id functioning as an ego; the most primitive national soul.

Juno's repetition of Mrs. Tancred's plea for human feelings rather than political alliances is an indication of the desire to unite the whole country by human features not political parties. Juno uses the plural form during her repetition of Mrs. Tancred's words, though the first version of the plea was in the singular, means that Juno is Ireland and not an individual.

Boyle's last words, which have become a proverb; "the whole world is in a state of chaos" are related to the myth; where trouble in the king's rule is reflected in trouble in the country. In Celtic belief, the king's righteousness is reflected in the prosperity and peace in Ireland. One could not travel easily in the forest during the rule of a good king because of the abundance of fruit and honey. On the contrary, when the king fails to come up to his duty, famine strikes the land and causes chaos (Monaghan 289). Moreover, it is also a Theosophist belief; the disorder in the psyche is reflected in the universe "… his material surroundings will reflect the peace and fraternal good-will which will reign in his mind…" (Blavatsky183).

Theosophy, being a complex mixture of beliefs, with the deep truths being secrets and the lengthy explanations of the same theme, made discerning the phases of initiation almost impossible. That is why the gradual initiation of the characters will not be traced in this paper. However, it might be that Mary's readings(Ibsen's), her contact with Bentham(Theosophist), going to dances(unity with the universe), music(otherworld and spiritual peace), explanations by Bentham (the Life-Breath and Yogi), the votive light(light reflects personality), Bentham's message conveyed under the role of getting the will (money is given to the needy through direct contact with them), indulging in physical desire (phallic worship), rejection of church and its representatives (emasculation rejection), the loss of parental control over the younger generation (disorder begins in the surrounding), funeral and party (violation of customs) successive catastrophes (disturbance in the surroundings to reflect the inner seeking self for peace), and mobility (violation of marriage bonds).

O'Casey presents Theosophy as an alternative religion to the two Irelands, which will enable them to be one nation. The individuals will be associated to each other by their humanity. As for religion, the church for O'Casey should not interfere with everything in the individuals' lives even in their primitive desires. In revolting against the influence of Christianity and the social norms in society, O'Casey liberates and unites the individuals who inhabit Ireland as a whole. Mary's violation of social and religious norms represents Ireland's rejection of these chains and slavery. By doing so, O'Casey does not discard national identity. On the contrary, he strengthens it. Celtic-Buddhism is older than Christianity in Ireland in addition to the fact that Christianity came from Britain.

Mary, with the attention directed to the name, is the Virgin. The Virgin rejects celibacy in Ireland. She wants to be impregnated by a person who worships sexual desire and not one who controls it.

Juno's prayer at the end of the play to Christ implies her desire for hearts of flesh to substitute the hearts of stone. When one controls his id to an extreme level, he feels that mercy is a weakness, sexual desire as the same, but violence and sexual desire control as features of a strong personality. Christianity, being the main reason of all hatred in 1922, makes Juno's prayer as a return to the true self by embracing the more merciful religion; Theosophy. The following quotation taken from a Theosophist's comment, can provide evidence and humor at the same time:

> The cruel, anthropomorphic and jealous God of the Jews, with his sanguinary laws of 'an eye for eye and tooth for tooth,' of the shedding of blood and animal sacrifice, had to be relegated to a secondary place and replaced by the merciful 'Father in Secret.' The latter had to be shown, not as an extra-Cosmic God, but as a divine Savior of the man of flesh (Blavatsky 57).

Juno's unusual endurance in front of the successive disasters which struck her family, can be explained with little suspicion to the interrelatedness between Juno's unbelievable spiritual power and the Theosophists' task "their desire was…to give the ignorant and the misled, whose burden in life was too heavy for them, hope enough and an inkling into truth sufficient to support them in their heaviest hours." (Blavatsky 55).

To conclude, the play from the very start to the end is about initiation of the characters in the Buddhist belief, which is Celtic-Buddhism in Ireland. This theme goes in developing as the play goes on until the end which accompanies the complete initiation of the characters especially Juno and Mary. Johnny is also developed and becomes a highly experienced Yogi. His death is the salvation from this world. However, his life has not ended, but his suffering in life only which has come into an end. Theosophy considers death as something not to be abhorred since it means rebirth in addition to the end of suffering in this life. Juno and Mary are well experienced in the new religion. They both reject the previous religious norms and revolt against the social norms, each by her own way. Boyle and Joxer are about to accomplish their spiritual development; this can be seen in them being aware of the general chaos around them, represented by the absence of any chairs, tables and other furniture. The death of Johnny and the deserted daughter in addition to the moving of the mother into a new place will add more to Boyle who will come to the complete self-realization. However, Joxer and Boyle are highly at the end of their transformation, and of course, in their psyches. As for Joxer, he seems a wise man. He shortens his speeches—though to mere quotations taken mostly from foreign resources—into simile and metaphor. This is an unclear feature of Theosophy, though. Theosophy uses simile and metaphor to convey its deep meanings. Even they think that the same words are heard by many listeners, only the experienced will be able to understand the conveyed meaning behind the surface reality. Moreover, Theosophy regards our language as insufficient to reveal the real beliefs concerning the Life-Breath, for instance. I would regret it if I did not quote one of Joxer's best quotations here, though it is well-known: "An honest man is the noblest work of God."

Moreover, he quotes one of Shakespeare's lines in <u>As You Like It</u> spoken by his British counterpart

> Touchstone. The more pity that fools may not speak wisely what wise men do foolishly.
>
> Celia. By my troth thou say'st true: for silence the little wit that fools have was silenced, the little foolery that wise men have makes a great show (I. ii)

The same line is repeated by O'Casey through Mrs Henderson in <u>The Shadow of a Gunman</u>:

> Them words is true, Mr. Gallicker, and they aren't. For to be wise is to be a fool, and to be fool is to be wise.
>
> Joxer. Where ignorance is a bliss it is folly to be wise.

By figuring out the general meaning of these similar sentences, one can see that O'Casey intends to say that the foolishness in administering to the needs of Ireland is due to the presumed wise, whereas in fact they are fools and the presumed fools are wise. In this way, O'Casey indicates that the middle class is better in administering the country's affairs and not the upper class. And the whole case being about national identity, this means that the real class which protects Irish national identity is the middle class or maybe the lowest classes rather than the upper ones. Supposedly, this is a fact; the middle class is the real chariot on which the development of the country depends in order to develop. In all the history of revolutions, the middle class and her less privileged sisters are the real makers of new a national identity. If they are not so, then, at least they preserve social customs and national aspects longer than the privileged classes. This idea is supported by the plot of the play; when Mr Boyle knows about the will, he ignores his neighbor's death and puts the responsibility on the government. When he is poor, he despises the priest, but when he is informed about the money, he tolerates the church's betrayal of the Irish and of being sentries over the Irish sexual potency. In other words, money made him less concerned with the nation with all its history, present and future.

By looking into the play equipped with more understanding of Theosophy, one can see the four noble truths symbolized in the play. Firstly, when the family hears of the will, they begin to crave. With this craving, the trouble increases. When the will turns to be nothing, craving stops. With the end of craving, Mrs Boyle leaves her home and husband, and goes with her daughter. She is in the eight fold path where she has right view, right mindfulness, right concentration, right resolve, right action, right happiness, right decision and right effort. These eight elements can be seen in the final decision of leaving, but since they come together, it is still difficult to distinguish one from the other.

When the two women leave, one can have in imagination two women and an unborn child. The child's mother is Mary. The child's father is Charles Bentham, whose religion is Theosophy. Taking into consideration that Theosophy is related to Celtic-Buddhism. The latter is a religion while the former is related to the philosophy of this religion. Celtic-Buddhism is the ground on which Christianity based its roots. Therefore, Charles is the father of Christianity. Charles Bentham is the father of the child. Now if one returns to the two women and the child, one can see that the two women are the two faces of Cathleen Ni Houlihan. The child— having two mothers, a divine father and the child's mother is Mary— is a Cuchulain and a Christ. When the curtain rises, the audience sees a picture of Mary the Virgin. Here is it at the very end of the play. Religion has been reformed to the level of being the same when Mary the Virgin was still carrying Christ in her arms. Cathleen Ni Houlihan is young again and she is expecting to lay down Cuchulain. National identity is at the best condition from two sides. Religion is reformed, and national identity is restored.

Moreover, when looking into the play again, one can see that the two Cathleens are two Irelands. One works and one is on strike. This is the situation during the time of Civil war. Mary had a relationship with Jerry for a while, rejected him and went to Bentham. This means the rejection of Labour Party for the sake of the Treaty. The child can be seen as a symbolic representation of the Treaty, but O'Casey does not condemn the Treaty. Bentham's quick leave to Britain is like the British withdrawal from Ireland. Before anything is settled, Britain leaves making a great chaos by this hasty evacuation of her forces. Mary, being rejected by her male members in the family, is to symbolize the refusal of the Treaty by some Irish citizens. Johnny being shot at the end is to suggest the end of murdering and counter murdering in Ireland. Robbie was dead, and now Johnny has followed. There is no need for more such violence.

The two women leaving the men behind or being left, is a complete representation of Cuchulain's and Christ's births. In addition to the two women being two Irelands, a Cathleen Ni Houlihan with her double face, and Mary is the Virgin. Therefore, nothing is left to restore of the national identity. All the aspects of national identity are now complete.

In the same line, one can add that the symbolic meaning in the play as a whole is the situation in Ireland after the Treaty, but during the Civil War. In this regard, it better to stress the theme of national identity. During the Civil War, a sect of the Irish was with the Treaty who were called the Republicans, and another party was with the independence of all Ireland. Both claim their truthfulness to the national cause. However, the child being celebrated by O'Casey means that he is with the Treaty. Even the Boyle family is divided between a supporter of the Treaty and against it.

The Plough and the Stars

The title is a reference to the flag which was raised by the Citizen Army in the Rising of 1916. A play about this military resurgence is related to national identity, though from a different perspective. This is related to the dispute about national identity; should it be mirroring the real or praising the mythical. O'Casey was concerned with the first type.

The stage directions in the play mention the display pictures of "the Sleeping Venus", "Robert Emmet", "the Gleaners" and "the Angelus". These pictures remind of many things. The Sleeping Venus reminds one of myths, Robert Emmet is a nationalist, the Gleaners is about harvest; realism or maybe socialism and "the Angelus" is related to religion. All of the mentioned ideas are related to national identity; myth, nationalists, peasants (realism) and religion. These are the features of the characters in the play. "The extended family of the Clitheroes includes an officer in the Irish Citizen Army, a young socialist, and a middle-aged Nationalist. Mrs Gogan's Catholic rhapsodies are balanced by Bessie's Protestant raptures."(Kearney 101) "While they exist as strong individuals, characters like Clitheroe, Peter, the Covey and Bessie clearly represent points on the political perspective: revolutionary Nationalism, obsolete romantic Nationalism, international socialism, and anti-Nationalist Protestantism" (Kearney 132). This is the Irish national identity which O'Casey tries to show from the very beginning of the play, conveying the meaning in pictures in the first place. Nora and Fluther are the two characters who respect all these diversities in the Irish national identity.

However, Nora is aspiring to have a better identity; first of all, by locking her door in front of her neighbours, and by trying to keep the place dignified as much as possible. This can be seen from her instructions to the Covey and Peter and also from Mrs. Gogan's criticism of Nora's behaviour. Nora is Ireland, trying to keep a comfortable place for divergent personalities, by making them respect each other. Nora, tries to shut the door in front of her Protestant Ireland sister. The romantic nationalist is in a continuous war with socialism. The socialist, again, is in dispute with Fluther, who has some respect for religion, while the socialist does not have this, and mocks religion and the religious. Fluther admires the mythical represented by the picture of the Sleeping Venus, defends religion, participated in a fight for the Labour Movement, saved Nora, and went home with Rosie. He is a "whole man" as Nora recommends him after he has finished fixing the door. He embodies the diverse national identity aspects in his personality. Clitheroe does not care much about any aspect of the national identity, except Venus, but when Mars calls, he rejects her again. Clitheroe was about to send Brennan to his way unless he was promoted. Aspiration, not self-sacrifice brings Clitheroe to the meeting. The same is for most of the Volunteers and the Citizen Army members. After Clitheroe has left, Mollser comes in to show the deteriorating situation Ireland has come to due to too much aspiration. The door is left open for the interference of the British supporter to come in.

In the pub, one can see Rosie Redmond, complaining about the shortage in men wishing to be with her because she is not able to compete with the rhetorical speeches from the mouth of the speaker. Rosie represents frank seduction of men away from their women. This picture is juxtaposed to the speaker alluring the men to go away from their wives so that he can achieve his means. The idea of wine being attached to blood and to rhetoric speech is highlighted from the very beginning; when Mrs. Gogan wonders what Peter was dressing for, Fluther replies that he is adorning himself for the meeting. Then, he reads the advertisement of the meeting in the paper, and says "well, they can hold it for Fluther. It's three days since I touched a dhrop, an' I feel a new man already." After that, Fluther and Peter enter the pub and drink. Later on, the speaker clarifies the link by assimilating the blood of battlefield to the red wine. Finally, Clitheroe and his comrades, before going to the battle, go into the pub and drink. Moreover, most of the ideas concerning bloodshed are linked to wine. Before it was a Christian belief, which will be explained later, it is related to mythology; it comes from Scotland, that the hero bathed his dead comrades with his own blood, to bring them great peace (Monaghan 226).

The speaker, being a shadow, is a reference to the fairies, who was thought to be able to kill a man by touching his head, and he would die by a stroke, which is similar to the cause of stroke nowadays (447). Therefore, the words are like the touch by a fairy; both are lethal. Moreover, the relationship between words in one hand and the fairies' touch/blood clot in the brain on the other, is established through the association of words↔wine↔blood. Or even words↔ blood ↔wine. To clarify the previous illustrations, one can add that poetry and words in general, were thought to have a magical power (Monaghan 200). The association of blood to wine is also a Christian belief, but used out of its context according to O'Casey. Christ drank wine to pacify his pains while he was being crucified, to redeem his followers from sin. This is the ultimate freedom, the ultimate self-sacrifice. However, the speaker is injecting his listeners with the side effects of his rhetorical speech—which the same are as wine—to make them go and sacrifice themselves by shedding their blood for his sake. Moreover, there is a woman, in Irish myth, who was enraged by the death of her father, drinks his blood, and goes mad (Monaghan 400). (This idea is to be used when Nora's madness is discussed). In Christian belief, wine is Christ's blood, and Christ is the symbolic father of the Christians. Here O'Casey used the symbolic meaning of blood to depend on the myth again. The Speaker is Rosie with little difference, but the importance is to the similarities. Both of them seduce, Rosie uses wine to counterpart rhetorical speech, uses body language to counterpart the rhetorical language, uses call for life to counterpart the call for death and uses earthly call to counterpart the heavenly call. Rosie is a complete version of Pearse. All the delivered speeches have historical reality. The speeches having a historical reality charged with heavy nationalist evocations is very national from two sides. First of all, calling history back is something related to national identity, and calling the personality by quoting his own words has a national dimension. However, these quotations are taken literally to re-evaluate their validity and righteousness. In the first speech, the speaker ends up the mentioning of all horrible things by crowning slavery over them all. Here, it is very national in the first reading of the play to see slavery as worse than bloodshed. However, O'Casey alludes to the speaker condemning himself from his own rhetorical speech. The speaker has enslaved the workers and put them under the charm of his rhetorical speech, injected them with an over dose of symbolic wine, and now they are ready to do whatever he wants.

This idea of rhetorical speech having so much power, might be associated with the belief that literacy was thought to be related to magic(Kearney 20).Here O'Casey wants to say that the real sacrifice is for the real causes of the workers not for Pearse's means, otherwise, the citizens are now sacrificing for Pearse. While the case was the opposite in Christ and his followers. The image of Christ's self-sacrifice and his resurrection was used in the whole of Europe at the time of the World War One (Kearney 120). Moreover, when one remembers Rosie's complaints about her need of more customers to improve her lifestyle to a better situation, it is necessary to think of the Speaker as intending the same intentions; using men to jump to a higher social level. In Celtic myth, the poet was given a high social level, but he had to go on training in the narrative, and memorise stories, then he would be promoted (Managhan430). Hence, Pearse came to these tenement dwellers to practise his instinctive eloquence for his career as a politician/leader, using images of Christ's sacrifice, but in a reversed way, and Celtic mythical imagery, conveyed to his listeners' mind-sets through the power of the word/eloquence/fairy's touch and wine. The whole image is similar to Nora walking in her sleep.

Fluther, commenting on his feelings while listening to the speeches, reports the strong effect of rhetorical speech on the listeners, and reminds the audience that this uprising is in memory of the dead; the dead, are believed to return to claim the living. If this is the myth, it happens in reality when all these men are going to be killed as a commemoration of the dead. Nora later expresses this idea which is reported by Mrs. Bessie Burgess, that "living things are dead, and dead things are living". This is also related to Celtic myth; it was thought that the dead could cross the borders which separate the world of the living from the world of the dead during some festivals (Monaghan 300). The dead mostly take somebody who is still alive, to the world of the dead.

Moreover, "drinking the blood would restore the warriors" (Monaghan 67). The first speech alludes to bloodshed as a "cleansing thing" while the second speech emphasises the fact that this military action is a kind of reliving both Christ's experience in shedding his blood to redeem his followers and previous martyrs' sacrifice. The Covey comes to the pub in order to drink and forget about the meeting, but he is accosted by Rosie. The Covey's upperosity/

arrogance makes him alien to the nationalists and the realists. Later, Peter and Fluther argue about religious affairs, to make it clear that everybody is more religious than the speaker. Peter went every year to Bodenstown. They are more respectful for the dead heroes; he brings a leaf from Tone's grave and puts it in his prayer-book. Moreover, it was thought that a tree planted on a grave, would be sacred due to absorbing the person's blood; drinking blood—the essence of life—restores the warrior.

Apart from this, trees in Celtic myth are believed to be sacred without being on a grave, and were divided in their sacredness. What is satirical is the fact that Christianity was suffering from the worshipping of trees and abandonment of churches (150) while Peter fills his prayer-book with tree leaves. Even today, some Irish still go and offer coins to the sacred trees (110). Mrs. Burgess and Mrs Gogan start to quarrel in the pub. This quarrel has something related to the outside events. Catholic and Protestant Irelands are at war with each other, and both of them have nothing to do in interfering in other countries' policies. Bessie rephrases the speaker's words by using Christian principles to justify the fact that her son is fighting with the British. Later on, Mrs. Gogan comes to physical abuse to avenge her insulted identity, which is connected to dignity and respectability embodied in her religious beliefs, and tells Mrs Burgess that after she is finished with her, she will have time to pray for her country and king. In other words, as the speaker can use religion to justify his deeds, so can the Protestants in Ireland—who are considered as betrayers—ally themselves to Britain depending on Christian principles.

The same religious principles are used everywhere in Europe, therefore, they should be, all, or none, considered right. Mrs. Gogan, leaving the baby in Peter's hands is something symbolic. Mrs. Gogan and Mrs. Bessie Burgess are the Catholic and Protestant Irelands respectively. The child, instead of having the two mothers, as his exemplar Cuchulain, is left in Peter's hands and later, on the ground. Putting the child in Peter's hands, one has to look at Peter's features; he is a romantic nationalist and religious. Therefore, leaving the baby in his arms is an allusion to a Christ-Cuchulain figure. Moistening the child's lips with wine, may be, is a reference to his Christianity and siding him to the Fenians. For the image of blood and rhetoric is well established. Fluther, after the women have been excluded from the scene, indicates that "there's no conthrollin' a woman when she loses her head" sure this is a natural statement if it is not put in the same line that O'Casey wants it to be in. the interrelatedness of woman/ Ireland is established very early in the play. When Mrs. Gogan indicates that Clitheroe has started to take things more quietly, and that the wonder of woman has worn off, Fluther says exactly

> ...Not wishin' to say anything derogatory, I think it's a question of location: when a man finds th' wondher of one woman beginnin' to die, it's usually beginnin' to live in another.

Therefore, up to this point, the speaker has used a technique similar to Rosie's, and fuelled national identity division in the country. The Covey tries to "show Fluther up" but in fact he is parading his "big brain". In other words, he sees his education as a power that nobody has its match, and that he deserves to be higher than others. The Covey tests Fluther's actions by testing him in the theoretical part of the Labour Movement, which he is excelled in, but cannot apply any of his quoted talks into reality. The Covey is a new speaker/Voice, who fills the listeners' ears with beautiful talks, shows off his Literacy—which was seen as tied to power in an oral society—and wants to be above everybody, doing nothing but ordering and theorising. He cannot apply his words to the real world, and even his words condemn him; Rosie succinctly defines the Covey's haughty way of throwing heavy words into the face of his opponent; she accuses him of composing jaw-breaking words, which he does not understand. The Covey's reaction to this statement is to deny Rosie the right to speak what she thinks of him, and he insults her dignity/identity. No socialist, as far as I know, denies a person the right to express his opinion, and keeps to himself the right to show everybody off, while he cannot tolerate being shown off. Again, there is a fight between ideal socialism and realism or even nationalism defending Ireland in the face of the haughtiness of socialism. Fluther stands in the face of the Covey to defend Rosie's/Ireland's insulted identity.

Socialism, being too idealistic, too theoretical, and uppish, Ireland has handed its insulted honour to nationalism. As the Nationalist Fluther wins

Rosie, so does Patrick Pearse wins the Volunteers and the Citizen Army. In other words, as Rosie wins Fluther, the real (nationalist, socialist, tolerating and brave) man, so does the speaker wins the most (nationalist, most courageous, and real socialist) men for his war. At the end of Act II, there is a song for life and another for death; one for the future and one for the past. Rosie sings of a boy "bouncing on the bed" and Clitheroe gives a command for marching. During Act III, one can again see Mollser, who is a lively example of the bad nourishment they get in the tenements. Moreover, she will have her role at the end. During this act, there are reports about the situation of the city; being ablaze, bombarded with heavy guns, stopped traffic, stuck citizens in the middle of the fight, shooting of citizens by both sides, and most importantly, looting. The incidents are reported accurately, especially the parts which are related to the G.P.O being demolished and aflame, and the declaration of the Irish Republic in the middle of this destruction. Shooting the citizens by the Irish rebels is also documented. Using heavy guns is also historically true. The looting is reported to be real at that time; the citizens exploited the confusion to steal/loot. However, looting contains symbolic referents.

    First of all, when Mrs Gogan and Mrs Bessie Burgess face each other during the looting incident, Mrs Gogan brings a pram, which Mrs Bessie Burgess tries to have. This is a kind of a dispute over a baby's cradle, a baby's cradle gives the hint to a baby's kingdom, and a baby's kingdom being the subject of dispute, refers to the quarrel between Protestants and Catholics over the would-be-king in Ireland. Every part of Ireland wants to be the homeland of the up-to-come ruler in Ireland. Moreover, when the two women come back, the stage directions are very helpful: "...Bessie is pushing the pram, which is filled with clothes and boots; on the top of the boots and clothes is a fancy table, which Mrs Gogan is holding on with her left hand, while with her right hand she holds a chair on the top of her head." Here is a completely looted kingdom; the chair is obviously a referent to an illegitimate chair to be taken by another person. Being over her head, and she as a symbol of Ireland, makes the image clearer; a looted thrown of Ireland. The table on the pram is another referent to a looted kingdom. The clothes of a supposedly an upper class property, adds to the whole image. Moreover, taking into consideration the pram and its significance, one can see that both of the women are kidnappers of authority. Later on, Nora loses her son and her brain. Attaching the loss of the son to the idea of losing one's mental stability, the walking while half asleep, a past memory stuck in the brain, and the eyes shining of insanity and looking inside directly give hints to Lady Macbeth.

If one goes to Celtic myth, he finds a woman, previously mentioned, who drinks her father's blood and becomes mad. Lady Macbeth establishes the link between the murdered king and her father by stating that she could murder him if he did not resemble her father. All this substantiates the argument that Nora is Lady Macbeth, and the legitimate king is her son, who will be labelled two other titles when discussing the coffin and its contents. When this come to the mind, one wonders where is Macbeth. He is Jack Clitheroe; " Jack" can be substituted by "Mac" and "Clith.." by "Beth". If this is not clear, it goes as follows: JacClith. Moreover, he is no doubt ambitious, and if Nora is Lady Macbeth, one has to search for the features that make Jack a Macbeth. This can be clarified in the following analysis, but now one has to return to Mrs. Gogan and Mrs Bessie Burgess. Mrs Gogan is obsessed by thoughts of death she has dreamed of during the night. This obsession is meant by O'Casey to refer to the belief that midwives were able to see the future due to certain features seen on the baby's body, and reflected in his life. Moreover, Mrs. Gogan mentions a strong woman who could lift a house on her head; this is an image of goddess related to prophecy. The prophecy, mostly occurs by slaying a human being, and while he is in death agony, he reveals the secrets of a previous death (Monaghan 100). This can be seen when Mrs Gogan prophesies Fluther's death during his search for Nora, during the Uprising and she mentions the opening of the corpse's lips:

> "…an' then, with a thrembin' flutther, th' dead lips opened, an' although I couldn't hear, I knew they were sayin', 'Poor oul' Fluther, afther havin' handed in his gun at last, his shakin' soul moored in th' place where th' wicked are at rest an' th' weary cease from throublin'.'

While Mrs. Burgess speaks three times during her sleep. In addition to the previous theme of looting, one can see features of Lady Macbeth in both of them too.

However, the whole featured Lady Macbeth is Nora Clitheroe. To push this argument a step further, Lady Macbeth participated in the assassination of the legitimate king. Nora Clitheroe participated in killing her own child. This is the legitimate king whom O'Casey sees suitable for authority. The unborn child is ripped off his mother's womb. This idea can be found again in <u>Macbeth</u>; Macduff was ripped off his mother's womb, and for this very reason—being not born of a woman—was able to kill Macbeth. When one goes to investigate the situation in the coffin, he finds Mollser and the unborn child in her arms. This is an image of Christ and his mother. Moreover, the child, being born by Nora and given to Mollser in the coffin, is an image of Cuchulain. To rephrase the whole picture; the child represents Macduff, Christ and Cuchulain. This is the complete national identity which O'Casey sees the Irish are in need of. The stage directions tell the reader that the coffin was put on two chairs. This is a reference to the two dead children inside the coffin; they are a king and a queen.

Bessie burgess nursing Nora is to symbolise and to report a truth; the symbolism is the nursing of one Ireland over the other. While the real fact is related to the Protestants sheltering the Catholics in their homes during the Rising events. Nora losing her head, is something related directly to the idea of sacrificing for the dead. When the whole nation goes on thinking of the past, Nora's mind sticks to a past event. At the same time, while she is a Lady Macbeth, she is Cathleen Ni Houlihan; Lady Macbeth's memory is stuck to the event of murder, while Nora's memory is stuck to the memory of Jack being alive, the baby and the travelling in countryside. All of these aspects make her a Cathleen Ni Houlihan. Moreover, when Fluther brings her back from her desperate search for Jack, he comments on her situation that she is "worn out from travellin'". Just to remind the honourable reader that her juxtaposition to Ireland was made very clear at the start by Fluther.

Mrs Bessie Burgess being shot at the end of the play trying to rescue Nora is something worth stopping to look at, though it is a scene of a lifeless corpse. Nora, crying for the dead, representing Ireland crying for her dead, and Bessie, representing an anti-nationalist representation of Ireland, goes to risk her life to save a whole copy of Cathleen Ni Houlihan and Lady Macbeth, is to subvert the idea of who is the nationalist and who is the treacherous. Mrs. Bessie Burgess at the end of the play sacrifices herself to rescue Nora. Before this, she risks her life to bring Nora a doctor. Therefore, Bessie Burgess is the most nationalist figure among the female characters, being all as different representations of Ireland.

This theme can be supported by Mrs. Gogan's speech to Nora, inviting her to lodge in Mollser's bed. Nora being lodged in Mollser's bed is a theme related to Cathleen Ni Houloihan returning young due to the sacrifices for her sake. This attachment of Mollser and Nora occurs directly after Bessie has been shot. Bessie died for Ireland, now Ireland can be young again. In other words, she is Cathleen Ni Houlihan but a Lady Macbeth too; Lady Macbeth becomes very physically weak, mentally sick and psychologically disturbed. This is Ireland after the Rising.

Now what can be guessed but not included in the play is that Mrs Gogan is the only Ireland left to look after the other part of Ireland, as being in urgent need of nursing. However, when one remembers Mrs Gogan's child, he becomes a little bit optimistic; the child, when Nora recovers, will have two mothers; he is a new Cuchulain again. That will be a difficult task assigned to Mrs Gogan; to look after Nora till she recovers in order to take a part in the breeding of the child. All the time before this takes place, Mrs. Gogan has too look after Nora and the child.

The idea of Bessie Burgess being a representation of Ireland can be found in <u>Gender and Irish Drama</u> by Susan Cannon Harris; " the female body becomes the sign, not of Ireland's invincibility, but of its vulnerability; it is not the ideal Ireland triumphant but the real Ireland—broken, bleeding, and dead"(Harris 218).

Nationalism for O'Casey, then, is self-sacrifice, but for the living not for the dead. Moreover, he sees national identity is a mixture of many identities; religious (Catholic and Protestant) nationalist (romantic, revolutionary and realist), socialist (idealist and realist) and realist. One can see Nora as having a secular identity; she does not refer to religion, does not care for anybody and unwilling to give her husband for the sake of revolutionary nationalists' cause. At the end, she is a mixture of two identities; Cathleen Ni Houlihan and Lady

Macbeth. Mrs Burgess is another mixture of two identities; she is Protestant, anti-nationalist and at the end, very nationalist with a mixture of a Lady Macbeth. Mrs Gogan, Catholic, nationalist and Lady Macbeth. The Covey, is Sean O'Casey himself. He is the socialist, but theorises too much in order to gain admiration and subjugate those who are around him; he does not have a clear identity too. He believes in socialism but he does not like to apply it. Peter is an obsolete romantic nationalist, who is too religious and does not do anything useful at all. Jack Clitheroe is revolutionary nationalist with a touch of Macbeth, makes him struggle for a clear identity. Rosie switches her opinions to suit her companion's, and in a real competition with Pearse, taking some of his men away to live, and opposes him by her body language.

The Voice, representing Pearse, is also a mixture of identities; he calls for military action depending on religious principles, then brings the memory of the dead to the front, mixing mythical, with religious aspects conveyed by rhetorical speech. Moreover, most of the characters lose their previously alleged identities during the play, and show their real identities. Surprisingly, all of the characters become more national at the end of the play. The previously alleged heroism and nationalism are swept away to leave the stage for real nationalism to show itself. Nora's ambition/upperosity, which is alluded to at the very start of the play, is depicted clearly at the end. Her songs during the honeymoon, given a natural context, are clarified at the end; she sticks to past beautiful memories, and wants to be out of the tenements. She does not like the present tense, it seems. She is either in the future, or in the past, but never in reality. Rosie is also trying to make her house and garden look more beautiful by bringing more companions to the house.

Mrs Gogan is always thinking of afterlife, or death. It gives her a "threspassin' joy" to be in a funeral. She lives in three dream-like worlds; dreams, past folk tales and afterlife. She rarely comes to real life, and if she does, it is just to show other Irelands'/ females' ills. Men are equally divided between real nationalism and real socialism on one hand, and romantic nationalism and idealistic socialism. The only character, who embodies the useful national aspects is Fluther. He is the only character who brings his words into action, though not always, but mostly.

National identity for O'Casey, to respect the folklore, religion, be a real socialist, live in reality and be brave. This is the meaning of the four pictures which the audiences see when the curtain rises.

The whole play can be seen as a psychic shock to the national identity of Ireland, and at the same time a shock for the citizens' psyches; when the psyche is shocked, the real psyche is shown, while the alleged psyche disappears. This is Freud's outcome; under pressure, the real psyche shows itself clearly. When Ireland was shocked by this unexpected uprising, the real national identity came into the sight/light. O'Casey saw this shock and the outcomes of it, and portrayed them in this play.

Language used in the play is Anglo-Irish. The dental stop realisation of /Θ/ and /ð/ may well be a contact phenomenon going back to Irish where the two coronal plosives are realised dentally, i.e. /t/ and /d/ are manifested phonetically as [t̪] and [d̪] respectively as in tá 'is' [t̪a:] and dún 'castle' [d̪u:n].."(Hickey 4). This pronunciation is found abundantly in the play. "dhrop", "dhrink", "thrimmin'","undher", "dhrivin'", dhrawn", "thryin'", "conthrol", and "wather". There are many other features which distinguish the Anglo-Irish language from the Standard English. The use of after to substitute the present perfect tense as in "bring it outside and show the people what you are after finding". The use of seen "we seen no sign of Nora". The pronunciation of you as yous when it is meant for plural. "There is no doubt that youse is common today in Irish English..." (Hickey 11). "Yous are all nicely shanghaied...". Some traces can be traced to oral culture; Mrs Gogan's remarks are mostly derived from the oral culture (Kearney 134).

When one thinks of the whole play, he can associate it with the traveller drama, but in an urban setting. In traveller drama, the outsider comes to a far place where he comes to contact with some villagers and leaves. During this short visit, the outsider and the community interact with each other and affect each other's point of view. If this can be applied to <u>The Plough</u>, then one can see that O'Casey meant that Pearse does not know much about the situation in the tenements. Moreover, the outsider is always seen as the saviour. This idea was adopted by the Irish at the time the play was acted in the Abbey Theatre; Christ shed his blood to set the humankind free from their sins, and so did Peares shed his blood to set the Irish free (Kearney 120). However, in the traveller drama, the outsider benefits from the villagers and leaves them, in most cases, psychologically altered.

When the uprising starts, everybody is an aspirant, and deluded. At the end of the play, things change to the better, although there is a great deal of damage in the outside world. The characters come closer to each other, help each other and use real language. Moreover, all the characters give away the pretended identities they had previously claimed. Peter cannot go to save the woman, who comes out of the blue to the house during the looting incidents, though he is a nationalist. Even worse, his mouth is wetting for something to loot, but he cannot risk the chance of being shot. All the characters go to loot. They are real people, in need of everything, and ready to risk their lives for something to wear, eat or drink, but not for the dead. The most obvious example of giving away the pretended identity is Captain Brennan's changing of clothes from military into civilian. Peter forgets about the sword, and the Covey is embarrassed by the British officer for mentioning Jerneskey's <u>Thesis</u>. Moreover, the startling transformation occurs in Mrs Bessie Burgess's treatment of her neighbours. When the play starts, Mrs. Burgess is not welcomed in Nora's house, but at the end, Nora "[is] in [her] own home". Mrs Burgess forgets about her own son fighting with the British, and goes to help a rebel's wife. This is the most wonderful theme that O'Casey implied in this play; for the first time in the history of Ireland, the Protestants are with the Catholics, in the same boat, against the British.

This statement is an historical fact; the British extraordinary violence used against the Irish during the Rising, made the Irish Protestants support the Catholic claim for home rule in Ireland. If this transformation in Bessie's psyche, one can remind the reader of the previous anti-nationalist attitude during the first two acts of the play. Bessie objects to the meeting, mocks the rebels and sings for Britain. Later, she gives milk to Mollser. Then goes to bring a doctor for Nora and nurses her in her own home. Moreover, Captain Brennan and the other men live in Bessie's home. Finally, she is shot by the British. Here O'Casey alludes to the fact that during the Rising, the Protestants, who are supposedly supporters of Britain, supported their own countrymen's movement. This made them under the pressure from two sides; the British were harsh to them for their betrayal, and the Irish considered them as supporters of the British, making them the most nationalist people in the country. Catholic men going to a Protestant church to be sheltered from the bombardment and to make sure they are under control, and the men playing cards in the church and eating, is something related to religious tolerance. When the idea is suggested, Fluther—the fullest national identity personality—is ready to show some respect for the church and wonder whether it will be all right to do so. Protestant Ireland is now dead for her role in defending Irish national identity. We are left with two Irelands; one going mad and stuck into the memory of fantastic past, and the other being Catholic, religious and obsessed with deaths. Therefore, Ireland's religion is Catholic, respectful of the dead, and not aspiring too much.

To have a new look on the four pictures mentioned or hanged when the curtain rises. The four pictures are " the Sleeping Venus", "Robert Emmet", "the Gleaners" and "the Angelus". The first one represents romanticism, the second is to represent history, the third for realism and the fourth is for religion. If Synge saw the case as levelling the gap between romanticism and realism, O'Casey saw national identity composed of two more aspects. Therefore, one has to look for the four elements in the play. Firstly, romanticism can be found when Nora is with Jack before the letter arrives. Romanticism is suspended due to the arrival of fanaticism. In other words, domestic romanticism is suspended for national romanticism. The first kind of romanticism is destroyed for the sake of the second. This is a national identity aspect. To explain how national romanticism was working to change national realism, there is the Figure in the window. During the Speaker's speech, national romanticism is conveyed by many vehicles. Firstly, myth is used in cases such as the remembrance of the dead and the need of warming the heart of earth with new blood, the connection of blood and wine (when Cuchulain's end came, his mother gave him wine to drink which turned into blood). More themes are also used such as the Fenians, the old warriors ripening the valour in a new generation. Another theme is the celebration of heroism as something celebrated by the Irish in addition to love of oral speech. Religious themes were also used such as Christ's sacrifice and his drinking of blood in order to pacify his pains during the crucifixion. While these aspects were present in the speeches, the other aspects were in the other side of the stage. Rosie is there in order to remind the audience of the suspended domestic romanticism for the sake of national romanticism. In her declaration of being unable to compete with the Speaker's words, she declares that romantic nationalism is more important than domestic romanticism. In other words, Rosie is there to represent the absent sides; realism and domestic romanticism. The whole picture on the stage, then, is nationalism versus romanticism. More specifically, national romanticism and religion represented by the Speaker, and domestic nationalism and realism represented by Rosie. Therefore, O'Casey did not attack Pearse, but he seems to be calling upon him to take realism and domestic romanticism into consideration. What one sees afterwards, is the two women fighting over a religious affair, then about respectability. The quarrel starts with the declaration made by Bessie Burgess of the necessity of helping Belgium if they are Catholics. The argument develops into personal one when they accuse each other of being ignorant of religion, being neglecting of religious teachings, interference with other people's doings, and finally whether their marriage is done according to Christian morals. By doing so, they use the normal religious beliefs known among the public, while Pearse uses the general ones. In this way, O'Casey presented domestic religion in comparison of political religion or national one. Moreover, they belong to two different sects; Protestant and Catholic, while the speeches used by the Speaker are more general and apply to both. Thus, the voice of the

Speaker is national in this regard. However, Bessie Burgess is there in order to present domestic Protestant religion in comparison of domestic Catholic religion, political Protestant attitude in contrast to Catholic political attitude. In this way, one can see that there is a relationship between the two women and Rosie Redmond. The women are at different sides concerning the Rising in regard of religious difference. Rosie represents realism and domestic romanticism. If one takes into consideration Rosie's surname, he can see a similarity with Redmond who opposed the Rising and attacked it as a treason of the Irish fighting with Britain during the Rising. Sure, Redmond did not go very far in this regard to the level of making him as a traitor, but only preferred to be with the British until the World War I ends. For the British promised the Irish to have independence if they fought with them in the World War. The Covey represents the sect which opposes the Rising on secular reasons. Peter represents romantic nationalism. In this way, one completes the whole picture on national identity during the Rising. However, Fluther Good goes to the meeting, drinks, fixes the door, argues with the Covey, helps Nora and Mrs Gogan, reveres the Protestant church, steals during the chaos and goes with Rosie. He is the only character who combines the most possible number of the divergent national aspects in his personality. Even his addiction to alcohol is celebrated as national; the Celts were known for their drinking of strong liquor.

When the play ends, one can see that the most notable changes are Nora's madness, Clitheroe's death and Bessie's change in attitude in addition to Mollser's and Nora's child deaths. Jack, leaving domestic romanticism for the sake of national romanticism, is granted what he went for; martyrdom. In this way, he is immortalised in the nation's memory. Nobody can say that even O'Casey would have underestimated the 1916 men's sacrifices when knowing that the independence was achieved as a result of these sacrifices. However, this does not mean that his decision in going into battle was only love for the nation. Clitheroe went to the battle for many reasons including the urge in him for promotion. But this does not mean that O'Casey is showing him as a traitor though he paid with his life. The theme of associating Clitheroe with Macbeth was done to clarify his ambition and not to show him as a traitor. Clitheroe's end, then, is the absolute image of nationalism. Nora's madness is portrayed as a shock over the loss of two of her family. She is the goddess of Sovereignty, who always mourns the dead as in <u>Cathleen Ni Houlihan</u>. At the end, she has returned young again, and the play gives hint to her recovery when the doctor tells the other characters that she will be "touched here [in the head]" because of the aesthetic injection. The injection and the ripped child are symbolic. The drug effect is known and is meant to symbolise the effect which the nation has to endure after the Rising. While the dead child is the expected saviour who was born dead because Cuchulain kills his own son while Cuchulain himself dies fighting the ghosts firstly, and then real enemy. Even more, Cuchulain is well-known why he took arms; short life for the sake of long fame. The child, being born dead is to represent the death of a national figure during the Rising. He is buried, but his mother will always remember him. His mother is Ireland/ Nora is singing songs of the past, about her love of Clitheroe cries for the child, and fancies herself in the countryside. All these are national identity aspects. The whole picture is realistic of Ireland after the independence. Two Irelands, one celebrates in new deaths and the other cries for the already dead. In this way, O'Casey associated the past heroes with the present. At the same time, he associated the countryside with city. By having two women, Mrs Gogan's child is the new Cuchulain who has nothing to do now, but to defend the borders only.

Bessie Burgess being dead, means Protestant Ireland has sacrificed herself for the sake of the Catholic one. In other words, other than this way, there will be no freedom. Having Protestant Ireland dead, means national identity in Northern Ireland is now dead, but for the sake of Southern Ireland. So it did not go without an outcome; national identity was revived in order to achieve national freedom, so being dead for the cause it was revived for is worthwhile especially when it cannot be helped. Mollser being given milk by Bessie associates Mollser with the world of fairies. The fairies, was believed, came to the world of the living in order to steal milk. Even the looting of clothes has something related to Celtic myth. Bessie, nursing and bringing a doctor for Nora is also associated with myth. The Celts believed that certain women, especially experts in birth situations, were stolen by the fairies in order to help the fairies lay their babies. When she opens the door and speaks to Nora she says:

There's th' men marchin' out into th' drhead dimness o' danger, while th' lice is crawlin' about feedin' on th' fatness o' the land! But yous'll not escape from th' arrow that flieth be night, or th' sickness that wasteth be day. . . .An' ladyship an' all, as some o' them may be, they'll be scattered abroad, like th' dust in th' darkness!

This speech contains mythical and historical implications. For the historical, the Germans, during the World War I, sent a message to the Irish army declaring that the British are bombarding your wives at homeland. The Irish men replied with shouting "God save the king". This allusion is also hinted to by Mrs Gogan when fighting with Bessie. As for the mythical, it is related to prophecy and druidism. In this way, Bessie Burgess is associated with the otherworld to the utmost level. For she prophesies two things; the arrow which flies by night and the scattering of the Easter Rising men. At the end, she is associated to the utmost level with the otherworld by going there. Bessie, being a symbolic representation of Protestant Ireland, meant that her death is the death of the Protestant religion and the death of national identity in the Protestant part of Ireland. More specifically, Bessie's death means the death of Protestant sect in Catholic Ireland and the death of national identity in the Protestant Ireland. This leaves the whole picture of national identity being Catholic, eager to talk about death and funerary rites, loving of the dead and countryside. These are the four pictures in the very beginning of the play. The play ends with the same meaning of the four pictures; romanticism/ national romanticism, heroism/ history, religion/ Catholicism, and realism/ love of countryside. These pictures can be reduced in their implication to mean realism and romanticism. This brings one face to face with Synge. The latter was the first to use the theme, but O'Casey made each one branch into many aspects. This is the second dramatist who believed in building national identity by bringing romanticism and realism into the stage. The final moments in the play are of the British soldiers having tea over Bessie's body. This is Protestant Ireland being under the British occupation. As for the dead body, it is national identity. When the play ends, one still has in mind that Nora is now at Mrs Gogan's home. More specifically, in Mollser's bed. National identity is revived, but the price is Protestant Ireland's national identity. Nora, being in Mollser's bed, is a revived Cathleen Ni Houlihan. The child is a Cuchulain, and Mrs Gogan is the Old Cathleen. The two women are Cuchulain's mothers. He is also a Christ-like figure in that he has no father, and being a Cuchulain, this means that the child has a divine father as his predecessor. In this way, pictures remain in our minds. Even more, now national identity, having all its heroes on the stage together, is very well. However, the whole picture is of two national identities; one Protestant (dead) and the other is revived to the utmost level. This is the case in Ireland today.

The Shadow of a Gunman

The play is about a period of Irish history marked by many military organisations. It is the time of Independence War. The troops used to supress the citizens were the Black and Tans, the Auxiliaries and the Irish Republican Army. The first two used to suffer attacks and guerrilla fights including ambushes (the play mentions one) by the IRA. The Black and Tans were ex-soldiers while the auxiliaries were ex-officers. According to an Irish observer the Black and Tans

> ... had neither religion nor morals, they used foul language, they had the old soldier's talent for dodging and scrounging, they spoke in strange accents, called the Irish "natives", associated with low company, stole from each other, sneered at the customs of the country, drank to excess and put sugar on their porridge (Ainsworth 6).

These features can be found in the play when the Black and tans come into Shield's room. Even the stage directions mention that when the word "whisky" is mentioned, one of the soldiers gives all his listening ability to the speaker of the word, and leave the room to search for it. They also know of suspecting everybody. This is also mentioned in the play during the investigations with Shields. Even the nationality of a person is taken into consideration. When Shields gives his name, the soldier says to him "Selt?" and the stage direction says that he means "Celtic". Another historical fact is the ambush. During the year 1920, the IRA made many ambushes for the Black and Tans and the Irish Constabulary in general. The bomb found in Maugire's bag is a historical fact. Even Shields says to Davoren that he suspects the neighbouring house to be a factory of bomb. During these years the Irish Republican Army used handmade bombs to perform attacks and ambushes. Moreover, during the investigations, there were lining of people, insulting words, the use of the butts of the rifles to hit citizens, the burning of houses, destruction of property and humiliations. All these aspects which distinguished the Black and Tans are documented in the play.

"To combat the Black and Tans, 'the Irish Republican Army split into small groups of fifteen to thirty men who used guerrilla tactics to keep their foes under constant strain. Many of its fighters lived on the run, moving continuously from place to place and seldom sleeping at home'." (Yun 208) So that is why the tenement dwellers mistake Davoren as "a gunman on the run".

The play mentions two rebellions "In September 1803, Robert Emmet was brought before British magistrates for the orchestration of a failed Irish rebellion, one that had come upon the heels of Wolfe Tone's own, larger failed rebellion five years earlier." (Perin 69). As for the mentioning of Emmet, he was torn between love of a lady and love of country, which makes his case similar to Minnie Powel's case. Even he became a legendary nationalist, and many poems were composed on him including a poem that became "a national hymn" (Perin 70).

In a translated version of the original Irish, Michael O'Faolain described the actual setting on which <u>The Shadow of a Gunman</u> was based O'Casey shared O'Faolain's one-room flat, the 'return room' as it is called in <u>The Shadow</u>, on the ground floor of 35 Mount joy Square for a period of five months in the winter of 1920–1…. It was here that O'Casey experienced the Black-and-Tan raid which provides the main incident for <u>The Shadow</u> (Grene 119).

Here are the historical facts in the play and now the analysis. When Minnie comes to Davoren's room, she finds him writing. They have a little chat before Tommy Owens comes to them. This little chat is important for it associates Minnie with Ireland. This happens as follows:

Minnie….I'd love to write a poem—a lovely poem on Ireland an' the men o' '98.

………………………………………

What's Mr Shields doin' with the oul' weeds?

………………………………………

Oh, aren't they lovely, an' isn't the poem lovely too! I wonder now who she was.

………………………………………

Davoren. Oh, that—that was simply a poem I quoted about the celandine that might apply to any girl — to you for instance.

In this way, one can see how O'Casey associated Minnie with the composed poems about Ireland by associating her with the celandines, and to any girl. By associating Minnie to the wild flowers, he makes her be associated to the land, and then generalise the type to be a representative of any girl. In this way, she is a complete type of Cathleen Ni Houlihan especially if one takes into consideration the mentioning of the 1798 rebellion. This rebellion is the setting which Yeats chose for <u>Cathleen Ni Houlihan</u>. Moreover, the worrying over the dead in the 1798 rebellion and 1803 rebellion led by Robert Emmet make Minnie Powel a complete version of Cathleen Ni Houlihan.

The play continues to make Minnie a Cathleen Ni Houlihan and a new quotation is needed:

Minnie....No man ud lay down an' die for any but a sweetheart, not even for a wife.

Davoren. No man, Minnie, willingly dies for anything.

Minnie. Except for his country, like Robert Emmet.

By associating the death for a sweetheart with the death for a country, the version of Cathleen Ni Houlihan, is supposed to be complete. However, this time the case is turned upside down; Cathleen Ni Houlihan dies for her lover and not the reverse. In the second Act, Seumus Shields satirizes Davoren and Minnie by saying "A Helen of Troy come to live in the tenement!

Later, Seumus foreshadows by arguing that:

It's the civilians that suffer; when there's an ambush they don't know where to run. Shot in the back to save the British Empire, an' shot in the breast to save the soul of Ireland.

Therefore, Minnie dies to save Ireland by dying by a bullet in the breast. When the blood smears Davoren's name, he is saved. Cathleen's blood this time is sacrificed in order to save one of the gunmen. The stage directions mention that Minnie shouts "Up the Republic" after being captured with the bombs. This is a national aspect in addition to the idea of self-sacrifice. What is astonishing is the close relationship between death and writing "every book is thy epitaph" and "the letter kills but the spirit gives life" (Kearny 69). This theme is found in The Shadow of a Gunman where the letter brings the Black and Tans and the IRA and the typed names "Minnie" and "Donal" bring Minnie's death. From this and Susan Cannon Harris' analysis (191), one can figure out that the play is about the power of the word to change the world. This is similar to Synge's Playboy. Therefore, comparison is needed.

In The Playboy, Christy develops his character through the power of his story to the level of being able to act his story. In The Shadow of a Gunman, the community must change due to the arrival of the stranger/ traveller. However. Davoren does not change, but he changes Minnie in the power of his story. Therefore, the power of the word to change the world, which a mythical theme, is used in this play.

The title being The Shadow of a Gunman, means realism versus romanticism.

The shadow is realistic, but the gunman is romantic. Minnie is attracted to the romantic, so Davoren hides the realistic with the romantic. Romanticism is nationalism, while realism is poetry. Poetry is at the same time romanticism. Thus, one has real romanticism and literary romanticism and both are national. The poet, in Celtic Myth, is the most type of people who are supposed to change the world by their words. Moreover, romanticism is associated with writing. Since magic is well-known to be associated with writing. Poets and magicians are most likely to change the world by the word. Davoren being a shadow of a gunman is national from both sides. If one takes him as a poet, he is the most expected character to change the world by his words according to Celtic myth. One the other hand, if he is a shadow of a gunman, it is national since he is supposed to be a defender of Irish independence. Now romanticism and nationalism go hand in hand. The romantic being national, this means the love relationship between Davoren and Minnie is national, especially when one takes into consideration that Minnie is Ireland herself. Minnie is willing to write a poem about Ireland and the martyrs of 1798. When she dies, the officer finds a piece of paper with "Minnie" on it and a blood spot on it. Minnie's blood erased the romantic and placed the realistic blood instead of Davoren's name. In this way, she has transformed the romantic to be realistic. She has turned the romantic nationalism with realistic nationalism. She substitutes romantic nationalist love into realistic nationalist love. All this due to a paper written on it the two names of the lovers. Since it is documented, it has the power to transform the world. This is the aura that the Irish put around the power of the written document. When the letter is discussed, a clearer glimpse can be seen on the power of the word as an example of the insertion of the word "shocking" into the letter. The letter and the piece of paper are romantic, and being romantic are national. As for the letter, it is directed to the Irish Republican Army. This is national from the view of point of the Irish. As for the piece of paper, it documents love of Davoren to Ireland. The hiding of bombs is highly national too.

The language in the play is the language of the tenement dwellers. Moreover, it is the Anglo-Irish style of speech. Here are some examples:

Seumus…..Upon me soul, I'm beginning to believe that the Irish people aren't, never were, an' never will be fit for self-government.

Mrs Henderson. …we better be makin' a move.

Minnie…..I do be on the watch every night.

Seumus. ….an' ever since I do be a –I do be a little deaf sometimes.

There is a clear avoidance of the present perfect tense when there is no alternative. Another thing is the use of the form taken from Anglo Irish style; do+be+verb/ noun. The use of seen is also a feature of Anglo-Irish. The use of the present continuous as a feature of Anglo-Irish too.

In a general look of the play, one can see that it is about a raid, and the consequences of this raid including the ambush. The raid is usually done against the nationalists, but the ambush is highly national. Thus, one has a national community being attacked by the anti-nationalist Black and Tans. The ambush is, then, highly national. However, Minnie dies because of the ambush and not because of the raid. Therefore, Minnie died in order to transform the romantic nationalism into realistic nationalism. The letter is intended to change the community's world due to the effect/ power of the word. The letter is burnt when the raid takes place. This means that due to the letter, the opposing forces of nationalism came to the house. Then, the unexpectedness takes the place of the expected. Even for the Black and Tans, the ambush is unexpected. This theme can be generalised to the case of Minnie; she dies by the nationalist hands she was defending. In this way, O'Casey intended to say that romantic nationalism is killing realistic nationalism. Or even, killing romantic nationalism in order to make real nationalism. This is the same theme found in Synge's Playboy. Romanticism is made realism. In this case, romanticism is parallels romantic nationalism while realism parallels realistic nationalism. In this case one can look at Tommy Owns as a romantic nationalist. While Shields is a realistic nationalist. However, the only character that develops from romantic nationalism into realistic nationalism is Minnie.

Being the representation of any lady in Ireland, or ever Ireland herself, one can see that O'Casey means that Ireland has transformed herself from romantic nationalism into realistic nationalism. Davoren, according to critics, is O'Casey. In this way, one can see that O'Casey intends to say that the man-of-letters' mission is "to put passion into the common people".

Romantic nationalism is found in Tommy Owens. Whereas realistic nationalism is found in Minnie. Minnie has transformed due the presence of the stranger/ Davoren. This transformation is from romantic nationalism into realistic nationalism. Therefore, psychoanalysis is possible here. Minnie was associated to the dead in her country, but later, she is tied to one of those she fancies as a stereotype of the dead. At first, she is tied to Robert Emmet, who is the father of nationalism. When she finds Davoren, she falls in love with him. Therefore, Davoren is a new copy of the previous father of nationalism. When she dies, she is tied to him with a piece of paper, which she thinks is very important. Moreover, Robert Emmet was torn between love of country and love of his lady. The same happens with Minnie. In her death for the sake of a new copy of Robert Emmet, she is engaged to the father of nationalism.

The Silver Tassie

The Silver Tassie is concerned with the World War II and its consequences on the Irish. The title of the play is taken from the cup which Harry wins during one of his football matches. This cup is smashed before the very end of the play when Harry returns from the frontlines after being hit in the spine. In a general meaning, the silver tassie means the Irish national identity. This idea can be explained by interpreting the meaning of this cup. First of all, it represents a victory in a Celtic sport; football. It also represents the ultimate level of physical power in addition to being a symbol for drinking wine and merriment. As well as the means by which Jessie is tied to Harry; their names were carved on it and both of them drank from it during the celebration of the victory. It is also a symbol of sexual power; when Harry is hit in the spine, he loses his sexual power and Jessie with it. After this loss, the silver tassie is tossed into the ground and broken. It also represents a glorious past memory of success. All these implications make the silver tassie a representation of national identity, and Celtic identity in particular.

In the following lines, the silver tassie is going to be a means by which all aspects of national identity are symbolized. When Jessie drinks from the cup, Harry kisses her. This is a connection of sexuality with the cup. Before the kissing, Susie mentions how Jessie is holding the cup, while her legs are visible to everybody willing to look at them. When the cup or the silver tassie is filled with wine, Barney uses taboo words to refer to the opening of the wine bottle:

Empty her of her virtues, eh?

....

Here she is now….Ready for anything, stripp'd to the skin!

In this way, the bottle of wine is assimilated to a lady and the silver tassie is filled with the wine of this bottle. In this way, the silver tassie is associated with sexual power directly. For the wine is filled into the cup and drunk. Therefore, the virtue of the wine bottle is drunk from the silver tassie. The cup, being a symbol of physical perfection and a symbol of victory in an Irish sport, makes the whole image associated with national identity. To elaborate this theme, one has to refer to the fact that during the Celtic Revival, there was a revival of the Irish sport to counterpart the English football: "the GAA [Gaelic Athletic Association] was also responsible for the development of the famous sport of Gaelic football, which became 'the most popular spectator sport in twentieth-century Ireland' " (Killeen 75). The silver tassie is a symbol of physical perfection which is an aspect in most of the Irish legendary heroes including the famous Cuchulain. Cuchulain is also like Harry proved to the best among his comrades in all fields of sports. There are many similarities between Harry and his predecessor Cuchulain including the winning of many labels in battlefield and sport, the responsibility of defending the country against the enemy and the attending of more than one lady. In addition to this, the silver tassie is a symbol of a past glorious memory of success. Therefore, when broken, this memory is shattered as are the pieces of glass. Then, the silver tassie's breaking is a shattering of a past memory. This means that the nation' memory is shattered. The nation's memory is the real reservoir of national identity. This lead to the conclusion that the shattering of the silver tassie is a shattering of national identity. Thus, the silver tassie is a symbol of national identity by being a representation of physical perfection and a symbol of victory in an Irish sport in addition to being a representation of sexual power (the Irish looked on Christianity as being a means of emasculation). The shattering of this cup is the breaking of the national identity.

When the play opens, Jessie is happy to handle the silver tassie, but when Harry is sick, she apologizes from coming to Harry in order to say a kind word. When Susie is left with Sylvester and Simon, she lectures about Hell and the everlasting torment in it. However, when she gets a place where she can exert her authority and pick up a suitor, she forgets everything about Hell and remembers only that everybody has to call her "Nurse Monican" and not Susie. She also advises Jessie to join Harry in the dance while she saw only Jessie's bare legs at the very beginning of the play. This upside down movement in Susie's principles and outlook into life can be explained as a kind of a flash of luck exploited to get rid of anything labelled as a principle or religion.

To start with the historical facts in the play is to mention that the British recruited many Irishmen during the World War I.

> Most of Kurlish recruits came from laboring class backgrounds and there was a general consensus that joining the army and accepting the 'King's

shilling' was seen as an opportunity to increase one's pay-packet as opposed to remaining at home with very limited prospects of a wage increase or even a job.... [S]oldiering was simply another job with a steady income and a pension guarantee at the end. Thomas Dooley has noted in the Waterford context that 'pay and allowances…provided many working-class families with a regular income for the very first time' (Karsten 3-4).

These historical facts are recorded in the play:

> Mrs Heegan. An' my governmental money grant would stop at once.
>
> ....
> ......
>
> Never mind Jessie's legs-what we have to do is to hurry him out to catch the boat.

Therefore, recruitments were taking place all over Ireland, men went to war for different reasons including financial causes. While women got the money for the absence of their sons and husbands. Mrs Foran's case is similar to Mrs Heegan's and she has to ship Teddy too. When the two women hear the "siren" of the ship, Mrs Heegan is relieved to ship the three men—Harry, Barney and Teddy—safely.

When Harry is hit in the spine, Barney is close to pick him up and later Barney gets a reward for saving Harry. During the Great War, many awards were bestowed to the soldiers. Another thing is the gas attack.

> Croucher. …Regarding gas-masks. Gas-masks to be worn round neck so as to lie in front 2½ degrees from socket of left shoulder-blade, and 2 ¾ degrees from socket of right shoulder-blade, leaving bottom margin to reach ¼ of an inch from second button of lower end of tunic.

These accurate instructions being given during the war and not before refers to the fact that the Germans surprised the allies with the chemical weapon. Alfred Owen, being considered as a literary figure is to be quoted instead of the historian:

> In perhaps his most celebrated poem, "Dulce et Decorum Est," British soldier Wilfred Owen captured in verse the horrors of this new form of warfare, a horror that he had witnessed firsthand at the front.

> Gas! Gas! Quick, boys!—An ecstasy of fumbling, Fitting the clumsy helmets just in time.

The play mentions the barbed wires in Act two:…[Across the red glare can be seen the crisscross pattern of the barbed wire bordering the trenched].

> During 1915, the Germans had constructed a defensive line of barbed wire systems, deep underground concrete dugouts and strong points, known as redoubts, along their front line north of the Somme (Irish 13).

Susie mentions her willingness to join in serving as a nurse:

> I go away in a few days to help to nurse the wounded....
>
> Women served as nurses in the Voluntary Aid Detachment in the front line (Irish 3).

> One British chaplain noted 'the astounding faith of the Irish' while another marveled that '99 out of 100 Irish would explain correctly Immaculate Conception.' ...Colonel J. E Nelson admitted that 'I used to envy my Catholic comrades their great faith.' A more recent commentator concluded that 'Certainly, the religiousness [sic] of the Catholic Irish... contrasts starkly with the mass of English soldiers, in whom religious feeling does not appear to be strong.' (Brennan 82-3)

This strong faith is portrayed in the second Act when the Visitor tries to light a match on the cross, one of the soldiers jumps and hits the match out of the Visitor's hand. Another implication to this historical fact is the portrayal of a ruined church at the front line in the stage directions which opens the second Act and here are some instances of these directions:

> Figure of the Virgin, white-faced, wearing a black robe....life-size crucifix.

When Harry is introduced, the stage directions indicate that "he is not naturally stupid; it is the stupidity of persons in high places that has stupefied him." O'Casey means John Redmond. For "On the 20th September, the leader of the

Nationalist Party, John Redmond, who was widely expected to be the first Prime Minister of the new Irish Parliament, called on the Irish Volunteers to enlist (Irish 2).

Susie indicates to Jessie that "…men that go with the guns are going with God." This indication is meant to echo Redmond's declaration that participating in the war is based on faith and religion.

After Harry's return from the front, he does not play again, mostly due to his injury and O'Casey alludes to the fact that "In 1905, the GAA introduced a ban on British soldiers and policemen playing Gaelic games (a ban not lifted until recently)." (Brennan101)

The historical facts being mentioned, one can go back to the play's central themes. First of all, the Irish participation in the War side by side to Britain makes Ireland a part of the British Empire. This is not contradictory to national identity at least when one looks at the thing from the Ulster point of view

> Asking 'What is Ulster?' Andrew Horner, MP for South Tyrone, answered 'It is a people not a place. We are a nation sprung from British stock, different in origin, in religion, in character and habits, in every ideal of life [to Irish Nationalists].... But we love our country just as much as they [Nationalists]do' (Hennessey 12).

Moreover, John Redmond, under the old definition of nationalism, would be a traitor;

> The divide between Redmond and the leaders of the Sinn Fein movement was of fundamental proportions, between Redmond's political nationalism and Sinn Fein's cultural nationalism. Political nationalism had as its objective the achievement of a representative national state that would guarantee to its members uniform citizenship rights, and tended to organize on legal-rational lines, forming centralized apparatuses in order to mobilize different groups against the existing polity. Cultural nationalists regarded the state with suspicion, believing instead that the glory of a country came not from its political power but from the culture of its people and the contribution of its thinkers and educators to humanity. The aim of cultural nationalism was, rather, the moral regeneration of the historic community or, in other words, the recreation of its distinctive national civilization. Cultural nationalists perceived the nation in organic terms, portraying Ireland as a living personality— Cathleen Ni Houlihan—whose individuality had to be cherished in all its manifestations (Hennessey26).

Then, for thinkers in field of cultural nationalism, every relationship with Britain is treason. Whereas political nationalists saw that the relationship with Britain is a kind of politics and the complete separation of the two nations is not beneficiary for Ireland. This division between political nationalism and cultural nationalism is portrayed in Yeats's Purgatory. Being this is the case, the research is going to take the side of cultural nationalism in discussing the remaining play.

Leaving the football team in order to enlist in the army who fights in the World War I is a kind of disjoining the cultural nationalist party for the sake of political nationalist one. Harry wins the silver tassie, Jessie and Susie. When he returns, Jessie and Susie are already lost and finishes the .loss by breaking the silver tassie, which he drank the victory wassail before leaving with Jessie. The destruction of national identity is complete. Harry's sexual power has vanished, his love and ability to perform Celtic sport, and the silver tassie are all lost.

Susi starts the play lecturing Sylvester and Simon about hell, but ends in Maxwell's arms. Jessie is described as being a girl of "twenty-two or so, responsive to all animal impulses of life. Ever dancing around, in and between the world, the flesh and the devil…Harry is her favorite…"

When Harry is injured, she sends a pocket of flowers with Barney Bagnal; her new fiancé. Mrs Foran's husband shouts to Mrs Foran that she has a "cheery amee…I seen you and her goin' down the street arm-in-arm…thinkin' of her Ring-papers instead of her husband. [to Mrs Foran] I'll teach you to be rippling with your joy an' your husband goin' away! There is also a scene of Jessie and Barney with her with the latter trying to undress the top dress of the former. During the Act II, there are many references to sex too. All these sexual indicative things give hints to Celtic-Buddhism as this belief is thought to be a kind of phallic worship. Therefore, it would be safe to indulge in this interpretation.

Susie starts the play with a religious tone, but ends in Maxwell's arms. In addition to Jessie's change of mind from Harry to his friend Barney. These hints refer to Celtic-Buddhism as this belief is thought to be a phallic worship. Harry starts with a sexual tone, and ends playing the ukulele. This change is towards Celtic-Buddhism away from Christianity as it best seen in Susie and Jessie's change of minds.

In looking into the play in general, one can see that it starts with the celebration of a football victory, continues on the front line to a hospital, and ends in the hall of the football team. Therefore, it is about cultural nationalism being interrupted by political nationalism. It mirrors the movement of cultural nationalism as opposed to political nationalism. Cultural nationalism, represented by Harry's silver tassie is won in the first Act. This trophy is put at home and Harry shipped to France. A symbolic silver tassie is given to Harry's soldier friend for his bravery in saving Harry after being shot in the spine. Maxwell gives Harry the silver tassie in Act one, and comes to test him in Act three. Harry is Jessie favorite boyfriend when he wins the trophy, but she is quick in changing him with his friend; Barney. Barney broadcasts Harry's achievement in Act one, but the people in authority announce Barney's valor. Teddy breaks the wedding bowl in Act one, but he is led by Mrs Foran in Act four. Thus, those who were in the peak during the time of cultural nationalism are the weakest, while those in the base during cultural nationalism are now on the peak. The whole play is about political nationalism's blackmailing of cultural nationalism.

Moreover, when one looks at the word "tassie", it is easy to substitute it with "lassie". Then, the whole thing is the representation of the silver tassie as a lassie and the latter to the nation. The nation to Cathleen Ni Houlihan and the last to national identity.

James Moran in his book The Theatre of Sean O'Casey argues that the play has similarities with two works of arts. The first is Alfred Owen's poem "Disabled". The poem mentions a former footballer who was injured in his lower part of body and is now on a wheelchair (73).

> He sat in a wheel chair, waiting for dark,
>
> ………………………………………..
>
> Legless, sewn at elbow, through the park
>
> ………………………………………..
>
> Now he will never feel again how slim
>
> Girls' waists are, or how warm their subtle hands
>
> ………………………………………..
>
> Now he is old, his back will never brace
>
> He's lost his color very far from here,
>
> Poured it in shell-holes till the vein ran dry
>
> ………………………………………..
>
> One time he liked a blood smear down his leg,
>
> After the matches carried shoulder-high.

>It was after football, when he'd drunk a peg,
>
>………………………………………..
>
>Tonight he noticed how the women's eyes
>
>Passed from him to the strong men that were whole.
>
>How cold and late it is! Why don't they come
>
>And put him into bed? Why don't they come? (21)

Thus, the similarities between the poem and the play are clear. The poem can be seen as very applicable to Harry's situation. The poem is published in 1919 whereas the play is written in 1928. The second influenced by work of art is Frank Hugh O'Donnell's play <u>Anti-Christ</u>. Moran contuse to indicate that there is in the play a character who runs into the dancing hall and tells the dancers of another character's madness. The same happens in the final scene of <u>The Silver Tassie</u>; Harry interrupts the dancers to remind them of himself. In Anti-Christ, the character answers the partygoers' indifference with a verbal attack. In The Silver Tassie, Harry insults Jessie and reminds her and her new boyfriend of a shower of kisses that Barney would not wipe away (Moran 74).

In this way, O'Casey has allied himself to the anti-war authors in the world. This is done as a reaction to Redmond's call for enlistment in the World War I in order to make Ireland a part of England, and to make peace inside Ireland too. In this play, there is a new kind of national identity; the opposition of imperialism and war in general. Redmond, however, saw that "…by fighting side by side upon the battlefield with our countrymen of all parties and creeds, then let us hope that when that day comes that never again will the old cursed causes of differences be able to divide us." (Hennessey 85) not only Redmond but also Stephen Gwynn called upon Nationalists to 'Keep [their] loyalty to the past, cherish the memories that can inspire [them]; but forget [their] hates; hatred is barren. Bury the **hatchet and take up the rifle**, for Ireland first, but for England also, and for the cause of freedom throughout Europe' (Hennessey 85 emphasis added). Thus the theme of political nationalism and its allegiance to Britain is well documented. O'Casey wanted to oppose this nationalism and adopt cultural nationalism.

The hatchet is referred to many times during the play. When Teddy breaks the wedding bowl, he uses the hatchet. Many times before, Sylvester and Simon indicate the usage of the hatchet during a fight. It is a symbol of Celtic weapons.

> This seven-centuried war was one of Ireland against England, nationality against empire, Celt against Saxon. . . . The struggle of nationality against empire is the struggle known for all time to the world. The result of empire is to crush out nationality, and destroy or impede expansion of individual national life. . . . The ideal state of progress would be the destruction of empire, and the consequent expansion of national life (Kelly 121).

This is the case in <u>The Silver Tassie</u>. Empirical power facing cultural identity. In the first Act, there is religion and Celtic sport. In the second, war and religion.

The third, one sees the war casualties. In the last Act, the celebration in the Football club hall. Therefore, religion withdraws from the scene as the play comes to an end. This theme goes to the heart of national identity in that the Irish soldiers are more religious than their counterparts in England. However, the substitution of religion with the party including the sexual references means a return to Celtic-Buddhism. For the latter is considered as a phallic worship. Whereas Christianity is considered as a kind of emasculation to the Irish. Thus, the celebration at the end of the play has some traces to sexual power which means a return or a conversion into Celtic-Buddhism.

Political nationalism called for the Irish to enlist. Therefore, Harry is nationalist in the eyes of Redmond and Ulsters in particular. The soldiers fighting next to the British soldiers is also national in Redmond's eyes. For he wanted to achieve Home Rule by siding with England during the war. Harry's situation after the return to his homeland is taken from Alfred Owen's poem " Disabled". This makes the play a mixture of history, literary influence, politics and cultural identity. All have been referred to, but we are left with politics and cultural identity. Ironically, both (politics and cultural identity) have the same objective; independence. When Harry comes into the stage, he has won the Silver Tassie, but when he is frustrated by the result of war, he destroys this trophy. This means that cultural nationalism represented by the Celtic sport, Celtic sexual power and physical power in general are destroyed by the war. This destruction led to the destruction of cultural nationalism. This might be read as an involvement in a war that is bigger than Ireland. That might be read by Harry's enlistment in spite of being a footballer and not a soldier.

The Silver Tassie refers to the ultimate success in a Celtic sport. In addition to the similarities between the two words "tassie" and "lassie". Also during the first Act, while celebrating the victory, Harry mentions words which apply to sexual intercourse rather than to the wine bottle. Even Jessie says " no double-meaning, Barney". All this refers to the Silver Tassie as a representation of Irish identity. By the end of the war, this identity is shattered. This act of breaking the national identity is attributed to Harry's loss of his sexual and physical power. Even Harry's friends leave him to watch the balloons released while he is playing the ukulele. Thus, the participation in the World War I has destroyed all the national identity aspects; the silver tassie and Harry's physical power.

Finally, what makes the play distinguished from the rest of O'Casey's Trilogy is the expressionism used in this play in addition to being influenced by other works of art.

Conclusion

National identity is a complicated matter and restoring it is not an easy task. Therefore, Yeats went to Celtic myth, historical events and Celtic-Buddhism in order to revive this identity. He conveyed the whole message through the use of poetic style of language in <u>The Countess Cathleen</u> and peasants' language in <u>Cathleen Ni Houlihan.</u> By doing so, he unified the Irish identity through many aspects; history, religion, language present, past, and future. He also associated Ireland with the universe through his dance. Even more, the future was associated to the present by prophecies conveyed by poets and other characters. The most difficult task was finding the themes that makes a convergence between Christianity and Buddhism or Celtic myth.

Synge was concerned with the deeper past. He relates Ireland to the Flood and its religion to the Celtic belief. He also connected the traveler with the sedentary in countryside with the latter being connected to the urban citizen. His language is the peasants' with the Anglo-Irish syntax. His most intriguing play was <u>The Playboy of the Western World</u>.in this play, he decided to make his words come into the real world before the audiences leave the Abbey Theatre. The audiences rioted against the play thinking they are protesting against it while in fact they were acting the same play themselves. <u>Riders to the Sea</u> is also wonderful in its themes of turning the glass upside down to mean turning Christianity into Paganism once again.

Sean O'Casey was concerned about urban circumstances in the tenements. He did for the city what Synge did for the country. He brought some mythical themes into the stage with the intention of bringing history back to the stage too. He showed how national identity is something complicated in <u>The Plough and the Stars</u>, where the real nationalist is thought to be a betrayer and the alleged nationalist is a liar. In his play <u>Juno and the Paycock</u>, he portrayed the half freed country being shackled by the same chains during the British occupation. He also provided a solution to end the ongoing war by rejecting the reason of this fight; Christianity and the CID.

In this way, Yeats was the real initiator of the revival of Irish national identity. Synge followed and took some themes from his predecessor in order to use them in his own way in their collaborative work to revive the national identity. O'Casey took from his two predecessors what suited him in order to use it in his own method for the same purpose. In this way, the three dramatists gave Ireland the broadest national aspects which can be revived or bestowed to a nation. Oldest religion, oldest inhabitants, oldest myths unity with the universe including the otherworld, unity of past, present and future, hatred of Christianity, the celebration of freedom be it national or individual, all this is conveyed by the least Standard version of English; either Anglo-Irish or peasantry or Dublin dialect.

What is common to three dramatists is something more than what distinguishes one from the other two. Yeats, Synge and O'Casey have the following features among them:

The theme of traveler and the association of this traveler to psychological transformation. The traveler symbolizes a visit to the past, or psychologically, the return to the id. This journey, though it is to the mythical world, is meant to be a step for the future. The theme of words being able to change the world is also used and even applied by them. Celtic-Buddhism and Celtic myth are main resources for the most symbolical aspects in the plays. Converging themes associating Christianity with previous beliefs are either purified from Christian reference or used for unifying the two religions. Unifying Ireland with the whole world is also a common feature among the three dramatists, but each in his own way. Finally, language varies from poetic style to peasantry to urban dialect, but what unites language use by the three dramatists is the avoidance of Standard English in favor of the more national language, be it poetic, peasantry or dialectic. Even in language, they have similar use of the same Anglo-Irish syntax in favor of Standard English.

Thinking of the Irish now as being very nationalistic, religious, unique in their dialect, offering coins to some sacred trees until this day and holding the real myths associated with each temple and strange-shaped stones are all related to the revival of national identity. Without those dramatists, national identity, if not lost completely, it would have been less than it is today.

Works cited

Ainsworth, John. The Black & Tans and Auxiliaries in Ireland, 1920-1921: Their Origins, Roles and Legacy. Cambridge: UP, 2001

Armstrong, A. The Playboy of the Western World and Two Other Irish Plays. New York: Penguin, 1987

Bell, O'Malley. Caehlin. Being Ireland: Lady Gregory in Cathleen Ni Houlihan. Ohio: Ohio UP, 2008

Blavatsky, P. H. The Key to Theosophy. Washington: Theosophy Trust, 2006

Boeree, George. Personality Theories. Shippensburg: Shippensburg UP, 2006. Original E-Text-Site:[http://www.ship.edu/%7Ecgboeree/perscontents.html]6/4/2013

Boltwood, Scott. Ed. Renegotiation and Resisting Nationalism in 20th-Century Irish Drama. Great Brtian: Collin&Cmith, 2009

Bramsbäck, Birgit, Folklore and W.B. Yeats: the Function of Folklore Elements in Three Early Plays, Stockholm: Almqvist & Wiksell Int, 1998.

Brennan, Eugene. Negotiating Texts and Contexts in Contemporary Irish Studies. New York: Syracuse, 2000.

Brennan Martin. Irish Catholic Chaplains in the First World War.Bermingham: UP, 2011

Burke, Mary. Tinkers: Synge and the Cultural History of the Irish Traveller.USA: Oxford UP, 2009

Clancy, Shae. Ed. Land, Sea and Sky.Cambridge: Up, 2012.

Cusack, George. The Politics of Identity in Irish Drama: W. B. Yeats, Augusta Gregory and J. M. Synge.UK: Ruotledge, 2009

Fleming. D. A Man who does not Exist: The Irish Peasant in the Works of W. B. Yeats, and J. M. Synge. London: Cambridge UP, 2000

Green, Keith and Jill LeBihan. Critical theory: A Casebook. London: Routledge, 2003.

Gregory, Lady. Cuchulain of Muirthime. Blackmask.Online.2001.

http://www.blackmask.com.1/6/2013

Grene. Nicholas. Synge: A Critical Study of the Plays. London: MacMillan P, 2000.

---. The politics of Irish drama Plays in context from Boucicault to Friel.Cambridge: UP, 2004

Grote, Georg. Anglo-Irish Theatre and the Formation of a Nationalist Political Culture between 1890 and 1930. Lewiston: Edwin Mellen P, 2003

Harris, Susan. Gender and Modern Irish Drama. Britain: Cambridge UP, 2002

Hennessey, Thomas. Dividing Ireland World War I and Partition. New York: Routledge, 1998.

Hickey, Raymond. Tracking Dialect History: A Corpus of Irish English. Palgrave: Essen UP, 2003.

Howes, Marjorie. Yeats's Nations: Gender, Class, and Irishness. Cambridge: Cambridge UP, 1996

Karsten, Peter. The Irish Soldiers in the British Army. UK: Peter Stern, 2009

Kearney, Colbert. The Glamour of Grammar: Orality and Politics and the Emergence of Sean O'Casey. USA: Greenwood P, 2000

Lee, Deng-Huei, The Evolution of Yeats's Dance Imagery: The Body, Gender, and Nationalism. USA: UP Texas, 2003

McCormack, W. J. Fool of the Family: A Life of J. M. Synge. London: Niclson, 2000

McGreevy, James. The Irish Great Famine. New Jersey: New Jersey Commission, 2000.

Monaghan, Patricia. The Encyclopaedia of Celtic Mythology and Folklore. New York: Facts on File. Inc., 2004

Moir, A. Michael. As Above, So Below: Doubled Plots and Notions of Aristocracy in Two Plays by W. B. Yeats. USA: University of America, 2010.

Moran, James. The Role of Women in the Easter Rising 1916 Was Written Out of the Record

---. The Theatre of Sean O'casey. New York: UP, 2013.

Murphy, John. Inventing the Concept of Celtic Buddhism: A Literary and Intellectual Tradition. Dublin: UP, 2010

O'Casey, Sean. The Plough and the Stars. Oxford: Oxford UP, 2000

---. Juno and the Paycock. London: Macmillan P, 2000

---. Shadow of a Gunman. London: Faber and Faber, 2000

Perin, Michael Jaros. To Have Lived is Not Enough for Them: performing Irish history in the twentieth century. San Diego: UP, 2008

Pamukova, Gordana. Constructing the National Canon in Ireland: The Function of Folklore in the Plays The Countess Cathleen and The Land of Heart's Desire by William Butler Yeats and Their Role in Strengthening National Identity. Canada: University of ST. Andrews, 2011.

Richards, Shaun. Ed. The Cambridge Companion to Twentieth-Century Irish Drama. London: UP, 2004

Ritschel, Nelson. Synge and Irish Nationalism: the Precursor to Revolution. USA: Greenwood P, 2002

Ronald, Schuchard. The Countess Cathleen and the Revival of the Bardic Arts. USA: South California UP, 1996.

Schulze, Inken. National Identity in the Dramatic Works of Yeats, Synge and O'Casey. Germany: Grin Verlag, 2006

Shakespeare, William. As You Like It. Lebanon: librarie du leban, 2003

---. Macbeth. London: Faber and Faber, 2001

Steiner, Rudolf. Theosophy: An Introduction to the Spiritual Processes in Human Life in the Cosmos. London: Anthroposophic P, 1994

Synge, Millington, John. The Playboy of the Western World. Oxford: Oxford UP, 2001

---. Riders to the Sea. London: Macmillan, 2013

Yeats, Butler, William. The Countess Cathleen. London: Thomas and Hudson, 2012

---. Cathleen Ni Houlihan. London: Thomas and Hudson, 2012

Yun Hunam. Appropriations of Irish Drama by Modern Korean Nationalist Theatre: a focus on the Influence of Sean O'Casey in a Colonial Context. Warwick: Up, 2010

Works consulted

Sweeney, Bernadette. Performing the Body in Irish Theatre.London: Macmillan,
    2008

Boyce, George. Nationalism in Ireland. New York: Routledge, 2004

Stubbing, Diane. Anglo-Irish Modernism and the Maternal From Yeats to Joyce.
    New York: Palgrave, 2000

Bechhofer, Frank and David McCrone. Ed.National Identity, Nationalism and
    Constitutional Change. USA: Palgrave, 2009

Castle, Gregory. Modernism and the Celtic Revival.Unted Kingdom: Camridge UP,
    2001

Winter, Horace. A History of the Celts. Great Britain: CPI Bath, 2004

Cleary, Joe and Claire Connolly. Ed.The Cambridge Companion to Modern Irish
    Culture. United Kingdom: Cambridge UP, 2005

Cleary, Joe. Literature, Partition and the Nation-State: Culture and Conflict in Ireland, Israel and Palestine. UK: Cambridge UP, 2004

Wheatley, Michael. Nationalism and the Irish Party. USA: Oxford, 2005

P. J. Mathews. Ed. The Cambridge Companion to J. M. Synge. USA: Oxford, 2009

Murphy, Paul. Hegemony and Fantasy in Irish Drama, 1899–1949. UK: Palgrave, 2008